Addressing Special Educational Needs and Disability in the Curriculum: Religious Education

The SEND Code of Practice (2015) reinforced the requirement that *all* teachers must meet the needs of *all* learners. This topical book provides practical, tried and tested strategies and resources that will support teachers in making RE lessons accessible and interesting for all pupils, including those with special needs. The author draws on a wealth of experience to share his understanding of special educational needs and disabilities and show how the RE teacher can reduce or remove any barriers to learning.

Offering strategies that are specific to the context of RE teaching, this book will enable teachers to:

- create a supportive environment which maximises learning opportunities;
- plan the classroom layout and display to enhance learning;
- help students of all levels to gain confidence in their reading and writing ability;
- stimulate discussion and develop thinking skills through using stimuli such as religious art, music, artefacts, film;
- successfully train and fully use the support of their teaching assistants.

An invaluable tool for continuing professional development, this text will be essential for teachers (and their teaching assistants) seeking guidance specific to teaching RE to all pupils, regardless of their individual needs. This book will also be of interest to SENCOs, senior management teams and ITT providers.

In addition to free online resources, a range of appendices provide RE teachers with a variety of writing frames and activity sheets to support effective teaching. This is an essential tool for RE teachers and teaching assistants, and will help to deliver successful, inclusive lessons for all pupils.

Dilwyn Hunt is as an independent RE adviser working in schools and for local authorities and SACREs.

Addressing Special Educational Needs and Disability in the Curriculum

Series editor: Linda Evans

Children and young people with a diverse range of special educational needs and disabilities (SEND) are expected to access the full curriculum. Crucially, the current professional standards make it clear that *every* teacher must take responsibility for *all* pupils in their classes. Titles in this fully revised and updated series will be essential for teachers seeking subject-specific guidance on meeting their pupils' individual needs. In line with recent curriculum changes, the new Code of Practice for SEN and other pedagogical developments, these titles provide clear, practical strategies and resources that have proved to be effective and successful in their particular subject area. Written by practitioners, they can be used by departmental teams and in 'whole-school' training sessions as professional development resources. With free Web-based online resources also available to complement the books, these resources will be an asset to any teaching professional helping to develop policy and provision for learners with SEND.

The new national curriculum content will prove challenging for many learners, and teachers of children in Y5 and Y6 will also find the books a valuable resource.

Titles in this series include:

Addressing Special Educational Needs and Disability in the Curriculum: Modern Foreign Languages
John Connor

Addressing Special Educational Needs and Disability in the Curriculum: Music
Victoria Jaquiss and Diane Paterson

Addressing Special Educational Needs and Disability in the Curriculum: PE and Sport
Crispin Andrews

Addressing Special Educational Needs and Disability in the Curriculum: Science
Marion Frankland

Addressing Special Educational Needs and Disability in the Curriculum: Design and Technology
Louise T. Davies

Addressing Special Educational Needs and Disability in the Curriculum: History
Ian Luff and Richard Harris

Addressing Special Educational Needs and Disability in the Curriculum: Religious Education
Dilwyn Hunt

Addressing Special Educational Needs and Disability in the Curriculum: Geography
Graeme Eyre

Addressing Special Educational Needs and Disability in the Curriculum: Art
Gill Curry and Kim Earle

Addressing Special Educational Needs and Disability in the Curriculum: English
Tim Hurst

Addressing Special Educational Needs and Disability in the Curriculum: Maths
Max Wallace

Addressing Special Educational Needs and Disability in the Curriculum: Religious Education

Second edition

Dilwyn Hunt

LONDON AND NEW YORK

Second edition published 2018
by Routledge
2 Park Square, Milton Park, Abingdon, Oxon OX14 4RN

and by Routledge
711 Third Avenue, New York, NY 10017

Routledge is an imprint of the Taylor & Francis Group, an informa business

First edition published by Routledge 2004

British Library Cataloguing in Publication Data
A catalogue record for this book is available from the British Library

Library of Congress Cataloging in Publication Data
A catalog record for this book has been requested

ISBN: 978-1-138-68376-1 (hbk)
ISBN: 978-1-138-68377-8 (pbk)
ISBN: 978-1-315-54435-9 (ebk)

Typeset in Helvetica
by Keystroke, Neville Lodge, Tettenhall, Wolverhampton

Visit the eResources: www.routledge.com/9781138683778

Contents

Appendices

Series authors

The author

Dilwyn Hunt taught RE for eighteen years before becoming an adviser first in Birmingham and then in Dudley. He currently works as an independent RE adviser supporting local authorities, SACREs and schools. He is also in demand across the country as a speaker on all aspects of teaching RE, in both mainstream and special settings. He is the author of numerous popular classroom resources and books and currently serves as the executive assistant at the Association of RE Inspectors, Advisers and Consultants.

A dedicated team of SEND specialists and subject specialists have contributed to this series:

Series editor

Linda Evans was commissioning editor for the original books in this series and has coordinated the updating process for these new editions. She has taught children of all ages over the years and posts have included those of SENCO, LA adviser, Ofsted inspector and HE tutor/lecturer. She was awarded a PhD in 2000 following research on improving educational outcomes for children (primary and secondary). Since then, Linda has been commissioning editor for David Fulton Publishing (SEN) as well as editor of a number of educational journals and newsletters; she has also written books, practical classroom resources, Master's course materials and school improvement guidance. She maintains her contact with school practitioners through her work as a part-time ITT tutor and educational consultant.

SEND specialist

Sue Briggs has been supporting the education and inclusion of children with special educational needs and disabilities, and their parents, for over twenty years, variously as teacher, Oftsed inspector, specialist member of the SEN and Disability Tribunal, school improvement partner, consultant and adviser. She holds a Master's degree in education, a first class BEd and a diploma in special education (DPSE distinction). Sue was a national lead for the Achievement for All programme (2011–2013) and a regional adviser for the Early Support programme for the Council for Disabled Children (2014–2015) and is currently an independent education and leadership consultant. Sue is the author of several specialist books and publications, including *Meeting SEND in Primary Classrooms* and *Meeting SEND in Secondary Classrooms* (Routledge, 2015).

Subject specialists

Art

Gill Curry was head of art in a secondary school in Wirral for twenty years and advisory teacher for art and gifted and talented strand coordinator. She has an MA in print from the University of Chester and an MA in women's studies from the University of Liverpool. She is a practising artist specialising in print and exhibits nationally and internationally, running courses regularly in schools and print studios.

Kim Earle is vice principal at Birkenhead High School Academy for Girls on the Wirral. She has previously been a head of art and head of creative arts, securing Artsmark Gold in all the establishments in which she has worked. Kim was also formerly Able Pupils and Arts Consultant in St Helens, working across special schools and mainstream schools with teaching and support staff on art policy and practice. She still teaches art in a mixed ability setting in her current school and works closely with local schools and outside organisations to address barriers to learning.

Design and technology

Louise T. Davies is founder of the Food Teachers Centre, offering advice and guidance to the DfE and other organisations based on her years of experience as a teacher and teacher trainer, and her role in curriculum development at QCA and the Royal College of Art. She led innovation at the Design and Technology Association, providing expertise for a range of curriculum and CPD programmes and specialist advice on teaching standards and best practice, including meeting special educational needs. Most recently, she has worked as lead consultant for the School Food Champions programme (2013–16) and as an adviser to the DfE on the new GCSE in food preparation and nutrition.

English

Tim Hurst began his career as an English teacher at the Willian School in Hertfordshire, becoming Second in English before deciding that his future lay in SEND. He studied for an advanced diploma in special educational needs and has been a SEN coordinator in five schools in Hertfordshire, Essex and Suffolk. Tim has always been committed to the concept of inclusion and is particularly interested in reading development, which he passionately believes in as a whole-school responsibility.

Geography

Graeme Eyre has considerable experience of teaching and leading geography in secondary schools in a range of different contexts, and is currently Assistant Principal for Intervention at an academy in inner London. Graeme is a consultant to the Geographical Association and a Fellow of the Royal Geographical Society. He has also delivered training and CPD for teachers at all levels. He holds a BA in geography, a PGCE in secondary geography and an MA in geography education.

History

Ian Luff retired as deputy headteacher of Kesgrave High School in 2013 after a thirty-two-year career during which he had been head of history in four comprehensive schools and an advisory teacher with the London Borough of Barking and Dagenham. He is an honorary fellow of the Historical Association and currently works as an associate tutor on the PGCE history course at the University of East Anglia and as a consultant in history education.

Richard Harris has been teaching since 1989. He has taught in three comprehensive schools, as history teacher, head of department and head of faculty. He has also worked as teacher consultant for secondary history in West Berkshire. Since 2001 he has been involved in history initial teacher education, firstly at the University of Southampton and more recently at the University of Reading. He has also worked extensively with the Historical Association and Council of Europe in the areas of history education and teacher training, and has been made an honorary fellow of the Historical Association. He is currently associate professor in history education and director of teaching and learning at the Institute of Education, University of Reading.

Languages

John Connor is a former head of faculty, local authority adviser and senior examiner. He has also served as an Ofsted team inspector for modern languages and special educational needs in mainstream settings. John was also an assessor on the Advanced Skills Teacher programme for the DfE. He is currently working as a trainer, author and consultant, and has directed teaching and learning quality audits across England, the Channel Islands, Europe, the Middle East and the Far East. He is also a governor of a local primary school.

Maths

Max Wallace has nine years' experience of teaching children with special educational needs. He currently works as an advanced skills teacher at an inclusive mainstream secondary school. Appointed as a specialist leader in education for mathematics, Max mentors and coaches teachers in a wide network of schools. He has previously worked as a head of year and was responsible for the continuing professional development of colleagues. He has a doctorate in mathematics from Cardiff University.

Music

Victoria Jaquiss, FRSA, trained as a teacher of English and drama and held posts of English teacher, head of PSE, music and expressive arts at Foxwood School. She became a recognised authority on behaviour management and inclusion with children in challenging circumstances. The second half of her career has involved working for the Leeds Music Service/Leeds ArtForms as steel pan development officer and deputy inclusion manager/teacher. She was awarded the fellowship of the Royal Society of Arts in 2002.

Diane Paterson began teaching as a mainstream secondary music teacher. She went on to study how music technology could enable people with severe physical difficulties to make their own music, joining the Drake Music project in Yorkshire and becoming its regional leader. She then became inclusion manager/teacher at Leeds Music Service/ArtForms, working with children with additional needs. As secretary of YAMSEN: SpeciallyMusic, she now runs specialist regional workshops, music days and concerts for students with special/ additional needs and their carers.

PE and sport

Crispin Andrews is a qualified teacher and sports coach and has worked extensively in Buckinghamshire schools coaching cricket and football and developing opportunities for girls in these two sports. He is currently a sports journalist, writing extensively for a wide range of educational journals, including *Special Children* and the *Times Educational Supplement*, and other publications such as *Cricket World*.

Science

Marion Frankland, CSciTeach, has been teaching for sixteen years and was an advanced skills teacher of science. She has extensive experience of teaching science at all levels, in both mainstream and special schools, and has worked as a SENCO in a special school, gaining her qualification alongside her teaching commitments.

A few words from the series editor

The original version of this book formed part of the 'Meeting SEN in the Curriculum' series which was published ten years ago to much acclaim. The series won a BERA (British Educational Resources Award) and has been widely used by ITT providers, their students and trainees, curriculum and SEN advisers, department heads and teachers of all levels of experience. It has proven to be highly successful in helping to develop policy and provision for learners with special educational needs or disabilities.

The series was born out of an understanding that practitioners want information and guidance about improving teaching and learning that is *relevant to them* – rooted in their particular subject, and applicable to pupils they encounter. These books exactly fulfil that function.

Those original books have stood the test of time in many ways – their tried and tested, practical strategies are as relevant and effective as ever. Legislation and national guidance have moved on, however, as have resources and technology; new terminology accompanies all of these changes. For example, we have changed the series title to incorporate the acronym 'SEND' (Special Educational Needs and Disability) which has been adopted in official documents and in many schools in response to recent legislation and the revised Code of Practice. The important point to make is that our authors have addressed the needs of pupils with a wide range of special or 'additional' needs; some will have educational, health and care (EHC) plans which have replaced 'statements', but most will not. Some will have identified 'syndromes' or 'conditions' but many will simply be termed 'low attainers', pupils who, for whatever reason, do not easily make progress.

This second edition encompasses recent developments in education, and specifically in religious education teaching. At the time of publication, education is still very much in an era of change; our national curriculum, monitoring and assessment systems are all newly fashioned and many schools are still adjusting to changes and developing their own ways forward. The ideas and guidance contained in this book, however, transcend the fluctuations of national politics and policy and provide a framework for ensuring that pupils with SEND can 'enjoy and achieve' in their RE lessons.

NB: The term 'parent' is used throughout and is intended to cover any adult who is a child's main care-giver.

Linda D. Evans

Acknowledgements

The authors and publishers would also like to thank:

Anthea Collinge, Dudley Wood School, Dudley

Christine Moorhouse, Castle High School, Dudley

Frank Bruce, Waverley School, Birmingham

Anne Mole, Kingswinford, Dudley

Heather Hughes, Cradley High School, Dudley

Carole Biggs, Educational Consultant

Lynn Openshaw, Behaviour and Attendance Consultant

Linda Raybould, Literacy Consultant

David Evans of Fox Lane Photography

Staff and pupils of St John's CoE Middle School in Bromsgrove and Queensbury School in Erdington for allowing us to use their photographs.

Permission to reproduce the following materials is gratefully acknowledged:

Daily Mail cover, p. 52, 'Playing God', courtesy of SOLO Syndication, London.

'Wall of Wisdom' (p. 53) and 'Mind Mapping' (p. 55) courtesy of *RE Today*.

Original line drawings by Iqbal Aslam and Jane Bottomley.

Introduction

Ours to teach

Your class: thirty individuals to teach – to encourage, motivate and inspire: thirty individuals who must be seen to make good progress regardless of their various abilities, backgrounds, interests and personalities. This is what makes teaching so interesting!

> **Jason** demonstrates very little interest in school. He rarely completes homework and frequently turns up without a pen. He finds it hard to listen when you're talking and is likely to start his own conversation with a classmate. His work is untidy and mostly incomplete. It's difficult to find evidence of his progress this year.

> **Zoe** tries very hard in lessons but is slow to understand explanations and has difficulty in expressing herself. She has been assessed as having poor communication skills but there is no additional resourcing for her.

> **Ethan** is on the autistic spectrum and finds it difficult to relate to other people, to work in a group and to understand social norms. He has an education, health and care plan which provides for some TA support but this is not timetabled for all lessons.

Do you recognise these youngsters? Our school population is now more diverse than ever before, with pupils of very different abilities, aptitudes and interests, from a wide range of cultures, making up our mainstream and special school classes. Many of these learners will experience difficulties of some sort at school, especially when they are faced with higher academic expectations at the end of KS2 and into KS3–4.

Whether they have a specific special educational need like dyslexia, or are on the autistic spectrum, or for various reasons cannot conform to our behavioural expectations – *they are ours to teach*. Our lessons must ensure that each and every pupil can develop their skills and knowledge and make good progress.

How can this book help?

The information, ideas and guidance in this book will enable teachers of religious education (and their teaching assistants) to plan and deliver lessons that will meet the individual needs of learners who experience difficulties. It will be especially valuable to RE teachers because the ideas and guidance are provided within their subject context, ensuring relevance and practicability.

Teachers who cater well for pupils with special educational needs and disabilities (SEND) are likely to cater well for *all* pupils – demonstrating outstanding practice in their everyday teaching. These teachers have a keen awareness of the many factors affecting a pupil's ability to learn, not only characteristics of the individual but also aspects of the learning environment that can either help or hinder learning. This book will help practitioners to develop strategies that can be used selectively to enable each and every learner to make progress.

Professional development

Our education system is constantly changing. The national curriculum, SEND legislation, examination reform and significant change to Ofsted inspection mean that teachers need to keep up to date and be able to develop the knowledge, skills and understanding necessary to meet the needs of all the learners they teach. High-quality continuing professional development (CPD) has a big part to play in this.

Faculties and subject teams planning for outstanding teaching and learning should consider how they regularly review and improve their provision by:

- auditing:

    a) the skills and expertise of current staff (teachers and assistants);
    b) their professional development needs for SEND, based on the current cohorts of pupils;

    (An audit proforma can be found in the eResources at: www.routledge. com/9781138683778)

- using the information from the two audits to develop a CPD programme (using internal staff, colleagues from nearby schools and/or consultants to deliver bespoke training);

- enabling teachers to observe each other, teach together, visit other classrooms and other schools;
- encouraging staff to reflect on their practice and feel comfortable in sharing both the positive and the negative experiences;
- establishing an ethos that values everyone's expertise (including pupils and parents who might be able to contribute to training sessions);
- using online resources that are readily available to support workforce development (e.g. www.nasen.org.uk/onlinesendcpd/);
- encouraging staff to access (and disseminate) further study and high quality professional development.

This book, and the others in the series, will be invaluable in contributing to whole-school CPD on meeting special educational needs, and in facilitating subject-specific staff development within departments.

1 Meeting special educational needs and disabilities

Your responsibility

New legislation and national guidance in 2014 changed the landscape of educational provision for pupils with any sort of 'additional' or 'special' needs. The vast majority of learners, including those with 'moderate' or 'mild' learning difficulties, weak communication skills, dyslexia or social/behavioural needs, rarely attract additional resources; they are very much accepted as part of the 'mainstream mix'. Pupils with more significant special educational needs and/or disabilities (SEND) may have an education, health and care plan (EHC plan): this outlines how particular needs will be met, often involving professionals from different disciplines, and sometimes specifying adult support in the classroom. Both groups of pupils are ultimately the responsibility of the class teacher, whether in mainstream or special education.

High quality teaching that is differentiated and personalised will meet the individual needs of the majority of children and young people. Some children and young people need educational provision that is additional to or different from this. This is special educational provision under Section 21 of the Children and Families Act 2014. Schools and colleges *must* use their best endeavours to ensure that such provision is made for those who need it. Special educational provision is underpinned by high quality teaching and is compromised by anything less.

SEND Code of Practice (DfE 2015)

There is more information about legislation (the Children and Families Act 2014; the Equality Act 2010) and guidance (SEND Code of Practice) in Appendix 1.

Definition of SEND

A pupil has special educational needs if he or she:

- has a significantly greater difficulty in learning than the majority of others of the same age; or
- has a disability which prevents or hinders him or her from making use of facilities of a kind generally provided for others of the same age in mainstream schools or mainstream post-16 institutions.

(SEND Code of Practice 2015)

The SEND Code of Practice identifies four broad areas of SEND, but remember that this gives only an overview of the range of needs that should be planned for by schools; pupils' needs rarely fit neatly into one area of need only.

Whole-school ethos

Successful schools are proactive in identifying and addressing pupils' special needs, focusing on adapting the educational context and environment rather than on 'fixing' an individual learner. Adapting systems and teaching programmes rather than trying to force the pupil to conform to rigid expectations will lead to a greater chance of success in terms of learning outcomes.

Table 1.1 The four broad areas of SEND

Communication and interaction	Cognition and learning	Social, emotional and mental health difficulties	Sensory and/or physical needs
Speech, language and communication needs (SLCN)	Specific learning difficulties (SpLD)	Mental health difficulties such as anxiety or depression, self-harming, substance abuse or eating disorders	Vision impairment (VI)
Asperger's Syndrome and Autism (ASD)	Moderate learning difficulties (MLD)		Hearing impairment (HI)
			Multi-sensory impairment (MSI)
	Severe learning difficulties (SLD)	Attention deficit disorders, attention deficit hyperactivity disorder or attachment disorder	
			Physical disability (PD)
	Profound and multiple learning difficulties (PMLD)		

Guidance on whole-school and departmental policy making can be found in Appendix 2 and a sample departmental policy for SEND can be downloaded from www.routledge.com/9781138683778.

Policy into practice

In many cases, pupils' individual learning needs will be met through differentiation of tasks and materials in their lessons; sometimes this will be supplemented by targeted interventions such as literacy 'catch-up' programmes delivered outside the classroom. A smaller number of pupils may need access to more specialist equipment and approaches, perhaps based on advice and support from external specialists.

The main thrust of the Children and Families Act and Chapter 6 of the SEND Code of Practice is that outcomes for pupils with SEND must be improved and that schools and individual teachers must have high aspirations and expectations for all.

In practice, this means that pupils should be enabled to:

- **achieve their best**; additional provision made for pupils with SEND will enable them to make accelerated progress so that the gap in progress and attainment between them and other pupils is reduced. Being identified with SEND should no longer be a reason for a pupil making less than good progress.
- **become confident individuals living fulfilling lives**; if you ask parents of children with SEND what is important to them for their child's future, they often answer 'happiness, the opportunity to achieve his or her potential, friendships and a loving family' – just what we all want for our children. Outcomes in terms of well-being, social skills and growing independence are equally as important as academic outcomes for children and young people with SEND.
- **make a successful transition into adulthood, whether into employment, further or higher education or training;** decisions made at transition from primary school, in Year 7 and beyond should be made in the context of preparation for adulthood. For example, where a pupil has had full-time support from a teaching assistant in primary school, the secondary school's first reaction might be to continue this level of support after transition. This may result in long-term dependency on adults, however, or limited opportunities to develop social skills, both of which impact negatively on preparation for adulthood.

Excellent classroom provision

Later chapters provide lots of subject-specific ideas and guidance on strategies to support pupils with SEND. In Appendix 3 you will find useful checklists to help you support pupils with identified 'conditions', but there are some generic approaches that form the foundations of outstanding provision, such as:

- providing support from adults or other pupils;
- adapting tasks or environments;
- using specialist aids and equipment as appropriate.

The starting points listed below provide a sound basis for creating an inclusive learning environment that will benefit *all* pupils, while being especially important for those with SEND.

Develop pupils' understanding through the use of all available senses by:

- using resources that pupils can access through sight *and* sound (and where appropriate also use the senses of touch, taste and smell to broaden understanding and ensure stronger memory);
- regularly employing resources such as symbols, pictures and film to increase pupils' knowledge of the wider world and contextualise new information and skills;
- encouraging and enabling pupils to take part in activities such as play, drama, class visits and exploring the environment.

Help pupils to learn effectively and prepare for further or higher education, work or training by:

- setting realistic demands within high expectations;
- using positive strategies to manage behaviour;
- giving pupils opportunities and encouragement to develop the skills to work effectively in a group or with a partner;
- teaching all pupils to value and respect the contribution of others;
- encouraging independent working skills;
- teaching essential safety rules.

Help pupils to develop communication skills, language and literacy by:

- making sure all pupils can see your face when you are speaking;
- giving clear, step-by-step instructions, and limiting the amount of information given at one time;
- providing a list of key vocabulary for each lesson;

- choosing texts that pupils can read and understand;
- making texts available in different formats, including large text or symbols, or by using screen-reader programs;
- putting headings and important points in bold or highlighting to make them easier to scan;
- presenting written information as concisely as possible, using bullet points, images or diagrams.

Support pupils with disabilities by:

- encouraging pupils to be as independent as possible;
- enabling them to work with other, non-disabled pupils;
- making sure the classroom environment is suitable, e.g. uncluttered space to facilitate movement around the classroom or lab; adapted resources that are labelled and accessible;
- being aware that some pupils will take longer to complete tasks, including homework;
- taking into account the higher levels of concentration and physical exertion required by some pupils (even in activities such as reading and writing) that will lead to increased fatigue for pupils who may already have reduced stamina;
- being aware of the extra effort required by some pupils to follow oral work, whether through the use of residual hearing, lip reading or signed support, and of the tiredness and limited concentration which is likely to ensue;
- ensuring all pupils are included, and can participate safely, in school trips and off-site visits.

These and other more specific strategies are placed in the context of supporting particular individuals such as those described in the case studies in Chapter 6.

2 The inclusive religious education classroom

Even before a child with special educational needs enters into a classroom where RE is being taught, there may be structures or traditional ways of doing things which may set them at a disadvantage. These are not likely to be deliberate obstacles. Quite unconsciously a classroom teacher may have developed particular ways of doing things which can result in some children being limited in the progress they can make. An inclusive RE classroom is one in which the teacher has identified what factors may place a child at a disadvantage and has taken all reasonable steps to remove those disadvantages.

One of the biggest challenges to the teacher of RE in establishing an inclusive classroom, particularly in a secondary school, is learning to know the children you teach as individuals.

Finding the hidden child

Teachers of RE in mainstream secondary schools often teach large numbers of children. The experience of many teachers of RE is a regular schedule of four or five lessons a day, for five days a week. Religious education lessons may last for some fifty to seventy minutes, with each class often containing around thirty young people. It is therefore not uncommon for these teachers to be teaching something like 480, or perhaps rising up to 630, children a week. The growth in the numbers of young people pursuing a GCSE full course, often beginning in Y9, has compounded the problem. There are now more young people in Key Stage 4 receiving their entitlement to RE but only in the form of a single weekly lesson. Specialist teachers in Foundation subjects like history and geography may well be teaching similarly large numbers. Nevertheless, it is a fair bet that the teacher that sees more faces in their classroom per week than any other teacher in the school is teaching RE.

Sixteen or more lessons a week, five hundred or more children to be taught, generate in terms of preparation and marking alone an awesome workload. And yet in among all that are individual children. Some of those children are specially gifted and have a real flair for RE, while some of those children have learning difficulties and could be really struggling. Regardless of what can seem like daunting numbers, the inclusive RE classroom has to have at its heart a teacher who knows each one of those children.

Consciously learn names

Some teachers of RE seem to be able to effortlessly learn the names of the children they teach. However, many more have come to realise that to do the job properly they must consciously make an effort to learn names. Any method or combination of methods, as long as it works, is advisable. A seating plan can be helpful, but others deliberately use mnemonics. Others find it helpful to use naming games which require children to identify themselves in the classroom, for example 'Who am I?'.

'Who am I?'

'Who am I?' involves giving a number of volunteers a 'post-it note' or a label which is attached to their forehead so that the volunteer can't see what is on the label. On each label is written the name of a famous religious figure, such as Moses, the Pope, the Buddha, Mother Teresa, Krishna, etc. The volunteer announces their real name and asks, 'Who am I?' The volunteer can ask twenty questions, to which the rest of the class may only answer 'yes' or 'no'. The object of the game is to guess the name on the label before the volunteer runs out of questions.

Other techniques for becoming familiar with names and faces include studying photographs held on school files. Some teachers of RE deliberately take photographs of the children they teach in order to cut and paste the child's photograph onto a piece of display work they have produced. Or a photograph of an entire class is kept in a mark book so that the teacher has a record of names and faces conveniently to hand, but can also learn the names of the children they teach at their leisure.

So much of RE depends on trust and the quality of the relationship between the teacher and the child. The teacher of RE, after all, is trying to encourage children to talk about their values and to share some of their most deeply held views and judgements. To do this the teacher must be able to demonstrate their genuine respect and interest in the child, and this is lost if the child realises that their name is not being used regularly and often, but that they are 'Thingy' or 'Yes, you!'".

Actively establish a relationship

Children who have learning difficulties often find that they can avoid embarrassment by becoming invisible. In other words, they don't put their hands up, they avoid answering questions, they don't volunteer information, they don't ask for help, and they rarely contribute to class discussions.

In the inclusive classroom the confidence and self-esteem of these children have to be raised if they are to achieve anything like their potential. It is for this reason that some of the most effective teachers of RE do not wear a mask which says, 'We are here to do RE business only'. They seek instead to actively establish a relationship by acknowledging children by name and saying hello outside of the classroom. They ask children about their interests and their lives and remember what they talked about. They might share a joke, accept a crisp and remember their birthday. They give gifts like a press cutting or a postcard which they hand to the child, saying, 'I saw this and thought of you'. Effective teachers of RE acknowledge that children live lives outside of school, and they attempt to build up a picture of the whole child. Often classroom teachers report that their success comes from the relationship they have established with children because they got involved in running the basketball team or setting up a drama club, or because they participate in geography field trips. As RE is about exploring children's inner space as well as the world of religions and non-religious world-views out there, any young person, whether they are a gifted learner or one who finds learning hard work, will respond better to a teacher they feel knows and cares about them. Although it might be interesting to be taught RE for a couple of days by a Robocop or a Vulcan, they are not likely to have much long-term success.

The learning environment

If RE is being taught largely in a specified classroom, most teachers will want to customise that room in various ways. Many teachers of RE will fill display boards with a mix of visual and written material. Some of this material will be commercially available and some of it may comprise examples of children's work, both written and graphic. Key words and religious artefacts may also be added.

This is all very well. Sometimes the effect can be very appealing, but all too often this is not the case. It is well worthwhile looking with a more critical eye at the display and asking, 'How can this environment be enhanced in order to support learning?' Frequently, the teacher being conscious of not wishing to appear biased, a little bit about all religions and perhaps some reference to a non-religious world-view is found around the walls. From an adult's point of view this is understandable. However, from the point of view of a young person with learning difficulties the effect can be confusing. Far from enhancing learning, the classroom environment presents a jumbled mass of data. In some classrooms, pupils are attempting to work in a space which threatens both cognitive and sensory overload.

Wheelchair users and visual impairment

Thought also needs to be given to the height and font size of any material which is displayed. Children who are wheelchair users simply will not be able to see display material which is set much above the level of their head. A large amount of commercially available RE display material often has text information which is little more than 12 to 16 points. For a child sitting ten feet away, print of this size is impossible to decipher. A child with a visual impairment, no matter how closely they scrutinise such information, remains excluded from a significant part of its content. Customising posters and graphic material with captions printed in a much larger font can help turn what would otherwise be little more than wall cover into an effective resource.

Display boards need not only be a visual experience but may also be tactile or even a multi-sensory experience appealing to touch, smell and hearing. Artefacts, such as Islamic prayer beads, various types of crosses, Buddhist prayer wheels, Hindu kum kum powder, Challah loaf, a Shofar (Ram's horn), a Salvation Army tambourine or a Kenyan church drum, can all, with the discreet use of fishing tackle, be safely attached to display boards.

Implicit religious material

There is also plenty of material from the natural world which raises important religious questions. A display of leaves not only provides a tactile opportunity for children with a visual impairment, but may also be used to reflect on the appearance of design in the natural world and how such intricate design may have come about. Forms of life in a dormant stage, like grass seed, an acorn, tulip bulbs, a coconut or the pupa of a butterfly, might be put on display to be touched and smelt, along with, if possible, examples of more vigorous stages of their life cycle. By doing this, questions may be raised about the origin and transitions of life. Questions may be asked about human life and whether we also perhaps transcend out of this life into another form of existence, the like of which we can only guess at.

Children with special needs often confuse one religion with another. One way of helping children with this problem is by separating information about the different religions and secular world-views using space and colour. One section of the classroom may be colour-coded using purple frieze paper, and this area alone is used for displaying material about Christianity. Another section of the classroom may be colour-coded with green frieze paper, and this area alone is used for Islam. Red may be used to colour-code Hinduism. Pale blue may be used for Judaism.

If it is the case that the class is exploring how two religions can be similar or distinctively different, the point can be reinforced through display; but do so by creating a separate display which is separately zoned. For example, children's awareness that what Muslims believe about the Prophet Muhammad is not the same as what Christians claim about Jesus may be supported in a separately zoned space. If this point appears as a display but is jumbled in among other data about Islam, it is hardly surprising that young people with learning difficulties don't get the point and are left simply confused.

The RE classroom should not bombard young people with masses of data, ideas and information and leave them to absorb it and sort it out. The teacher of RE should help young people to develop a mental construct of what a religion is about. This is done by providing children with a manageable number of key ideas or beliefs set in the context of a particular religion. These key ideas may be displayed in a classroom with the fundamental points indicated that are to be learnt at this stage. This material may be presented in a large font which the pupils can read from anywhere in the classroom. By doing so, key messages about a religion can be pressed home and reinforced in order to establish confident and secure learning.

Let's look at an example of this in practice. During a series of lessons about the Jewish Sabbath, the Shabbat, the children might be asked to suggest not only what Jews do on the Sabbath but why the day is so important. There are many answers to that question. The Sabbath is important because:

* keeping the Sabbath is a requirement in the Torah;
* the Sabbath recalls events associated with the Exodus;
* it is a reminder of the story of God's creation;
* it is an ancient Jewish tradition;
* it provides a regular welcome break from the routine of life.

Given the complex and subtle nature of religion, all of these answers are true. As the question is being explored, one boy whose reading and writing skills are very limited but who has a flair for a vivid metaphor suggests, 'It's the glue that keeps them together.'

This is a moment of serendipity in the RE classroom. The classroom display might well show a large poster of a Jewish family celebrating the Sabbath. It may well have information about the candles, the bread, the wine, but in 350 mm font are the words: 'It's the glue that keeps them together.' There is no pretence that this is a full or complete answer. What it offers, though, is a clear and precise piece of learning that pupils can retain. It also affirms the self-esteem of the originator and sends a message to all learners that their ideas will be recognised and their contributions valued.

For some students, avoiding confusing them with too much information is particularly necessary. For example, for children that are on the autistic spectrum, although visual clues are important, it may be just as important to avoid visual data overload. Visual distractions and smells may unsettle a pupil. In some cases a visual barrier or even a study carrel may be helpful in order to enable pupils to cope more effectively with their hyper-sensitivity.

The value of using material drawn from the natural world has already been referred to. Powerful visual images such as a sunrise, a magnified snowflake or a view of earth from space, accompanied by questions like 'Is there a spiritual being that created this?', 'Are there signs of God in the universe?', 'What are we doing here?', 'Have we been created for a purpose?', serve as reminders of the profound and enduring questions which religious education at its best seeks to engage with. Newspaper cuttings about events like floods or earthquakes, or news items which raise ethical issues such as crime reports, medical procedures or scientific research, all help to make it clear that religion is relevant and contemporary.

Example

Large and prominent messages, for example 30 cm high letters spelling out the word 'THINK', can provide a permanent reminder to pupils that there is an expectation that they should voice their own ideas. A giant ear with the word 'LISTEN' printed underneath reinforces the message that RE discussion is not about scoring points but is about listening to what others have to say and taking this into account as pupils form their view.

In order to help children to learn in RE it is helpful to provide permanent reminders of the aim of the subject. The suspicion some children may have, even though the point may have been made earlier, is to think RE is really about encouraging faith and attempting to nurture pupils into having a faith commitment. The teacher of RE needs to create a learning environment which makes it clear that RE is about exploring, understanding, questioning and thinking and is not about violating the child's right to their views or indoctrinating them into a religious faith. Similar support can be given to pupils' understanding of the subject and their awareness of why RE is being taught by prominently displaying quotations which affirm the educational purpose and value of the subject. Suitable quotations may be found in the local agreed syllabus which the school is required to follow. Or alternatively leading RE experts may also be used as a source of quotations which express the true value of the subject.

Wall of Wisdom

A Wall of Wisdom is an identified space in the classroom on which a record is kept of some of the more startling and thoughtful comments made by pupils in the school in response to life in general and to religious and non-religious world-views in particular. Young people often come up with remarkable and fascinating statements. Sometimes pupils may say things as part of a discussion, or as a response to something that has happened to them or they have heard about in the news, or sometimes, seemingly out of nowhere, children can say things which raise a difficult question or bring fresh insight. Not unlike the brazen comment of the child in the story 'The Emperor's New Clothes', children say things like:

'Where do all the dead people go?'
'Why are some people so 'orrible – I don't think they mean to be?'
'God is everywhere like the air you breathe.'
'Life is like a long journey.'
'If God made the world, who made God?'
'Why do some religious people hate other people?'
'The best time to pray is when it is quiet and you need God.'
'People are scared of what they don't know.'
'Why did Gran have to die when we loved her?'

Instead of questions and statements being lost forever, the teacher records them onto large speech bubbles which are then displayed on the Wall of Wisdom. The name of the child, their class and the date are also recorded on the bubble. If they have no objection, the speech bubble can be further personalised by adding a photograph of the child.

Figure 1.1 Umair points to his question on the Wall of Wisdom

See: RE Today *16/3 (Summer 1999)*

As the comments on the Wall come from the children, it can be particularly rewarding for young people who have reading and writing difficulties to find themselves being listened to and affirmed in this way. Also it provides a message to young people that RE isn't just about organised religion or what grown-ups think. RE is also about them, their experiences of the world and how they attempt to make sense of life.

Classroom layout

Seating arrangements for RE classrooms have been a subject of discussion for many years. As well as the obvious requirements, for example making sure that there is enough space for all pupils, including wheelchair users, and support staff to sit and move about, there is certainly a lot to be said for giving serious thought to how seating affects the social dynamics of a classroom, and how it supports some activities and limits others. In the influential book *New Methods in RE Teaching*, the experience of teachers that make widespread use of kinaesthetic activities and discussion was that traditional rows of desks confined both them and their pupils. Teachers rearranged the furniture in their classrooms by placing desks so that they lined the outside walls. Chairs were arranged to face outwards for written work, but they could easily be turned inwards, making a horseshoe or circle, for discussion.

Not all teachers will find it practical to arrange their RE classroom in this way and not all teachers, even if they could, would feel comfortable with this layout. Nevertheless, having children seated behind desks in rows facing towards the teacher signals that the teacher is the dominant voice in the classroom and that children's comments are to be largely directed through the teacher. More genuine and vibrant class discussion which involves reciprocal discussion, that is, pupil-to-pupil exchanges and not just pupil-to-teacher exchanges, is extremely difficult for children unless they can face each other and see each other's reactions, as is possible when sitting in a circle. Even if the set-up isn't permanent, the mark of an inclusive RE classroom is flexibility, so that pupils can relatively easily form a discussion circle.

Group work

Flexibility is also needed in the RE classroom so that group work can regularly take place. Groups enable pupils to learn from each other, try out ideas and gain confidence. They provide opportunities to learn to cooperate and work together as a team. Friendship groups are an obvious arrangement; however, this should not be the only arrangement in the RE classroom. Putting pupils together who don't normally relate well reinforces important aims. A central part of RE is for pupils to recognise differences and learn to respect diversity. Children shouldn't just talk about diversity theoretically. They should have opportunities to express their own views and to hear alternative, and perhaps contradictory, views of others and to do so in the relatively safe environment of the classroom.

This can be planned by the teacher, or on some occasions children may be randomly paired in order to encourage young people to interact with others in the classroom with whom they hardly socialise. Games like 'Find your partner', which involves the pupils randomly picking a paper on which is written a well-known character or person, e.g. Harry Potter, Ron Weasley, Romeo, Juliet, Hansel, Gretel, Bilbo Baggins, Sam Gamgee, Batman, Robin, generate a sense of fun in the classroom and can help combat feelings of nervousness or tension. (See Appendix 5 for advice on turn-taking. Where pupils find it difficult to wait for their turn, try the circle-time approach of passing around an object – only the person holding the object can speak.)

Literacy skills

The teacher of RE will often find in their classroom a wide diversity of literacy skills. Some pupils may be very skilful readers and writers, while others may have real difficulty, resulting in 'writing apprehension'. Writing apprehension can often lead to pupils adopting strategies to avoid writing and, with little practice at writing, this in turn leads to a cycle of failure. The approach of some teachers is to follow a line of least resistance. Writing activities are kept to a minimum, and where they are used they tend to be very simplistic. Composition is largely avoided, and instead pupils' writing is mostly limited to lists, labels, bullet-pointed notes, word searches, single-word answers or cloze activities.

Although speaking and listening skills are very important, so also are the skills of reading and writing, and the RE classroom has an important role in helping children to gain more confidence and raise their level of achievement. The improvement of writing skills requires teachers of RE to do more than set writing tasks for children and be encouraging and enthusiastic. Writing is the most demanding of all language skills. Pupils have difficulty not only with the mechanical aspects of writing, such as handwriting, spelling and punctuation; they may also have a problem with composition, or having something to say, and find it difficult to plan, sequence ideas, edit and revise their work.

To help young people make progress, the following are some suggestions:

- **Demonstrate the writing process** – this involves the teacher modelling the process of composition. The teacher provides a commentary on how ideas may be organised and how early stages from talk to notes, to eventually formal writing, may take place.

- **Shared composition** – this involves the pupils themselves largely undertaking the composition and the editing process, with the teacher serving as a scribe.
- **Supported writing** – the pupils work using the help provided by a writing frame (see Appendix 8 for an example of an RE writing frame) but with additional supportive strategies such as a writing partner or suggesting key words appropriate to the given assignment.
- **Diagnostic support** – some children that have difficulty with writing do so partly because they have a particular recurring weakness. For example, some children use long rambling sentences with repetitive use of conjunctions ('and then they pray and then they hear the Bible and then they all stand up') or repeatedly misspell the same words (e.g. 'beleve', 'Jewes', 'becuse'). Such difficulties need to be homed in on and the children actively supported so that the problem can be overcome. (See Appendix 6 for notes on spelling.)
- **Prepare for writing** – help pupils to generate ideas and record them through preliminary discussion, brainstorming, mind-mapping, visualising, identifying analogies, metaphors and key words.

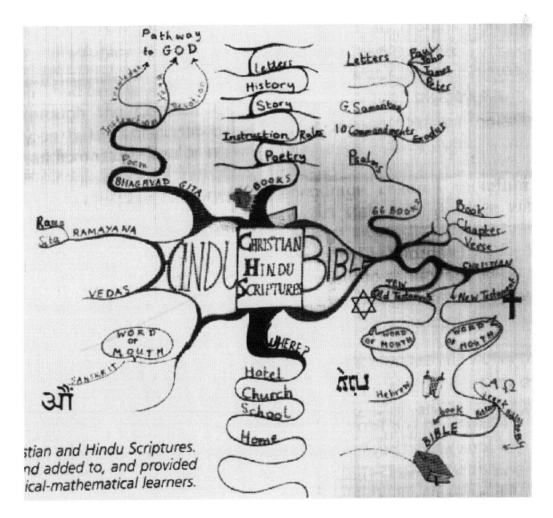

Figure 1.2 Mind Mapping.

See: RE Today *20/3 (Summer 2003)*

- **Make writing exciting** – often writing activities in RE are rather formal, if not dull; for example, a not untypical writing activity used in RE might be a task such as 'Describe what is said and done at an infant baptism'. Try to pep up the activity and give children a motive for writing by introducing a setting, an audience, novelty and a source of amusement, e.g. 'An alien cultural observer called Xyglubb, from a distant galaxy, observes an infant baptism. He has decided to send an intergalactic text message to his home planet. He begins: "I've discovered that these disgusting earthlings try to drown their children. In a ghastly ceremony . . ." Help Xyglubb write the message so that he doesn't get into trouble.'

- **Drafting and redrafting** – few people can produce a sustained piece of fluent writing in a single draft. Give pupils an opportunity to learn from their first effort and return to the task in order to improve the work and polish their own writing. Word processing can be of great help to pupils in this process, as it enables pupils to redraft a work many times, eventually ending up with a product they can take pride in and perhaps have published in some form. Software such as Clicker 7 (Crick Software) is very supportive to pupils who find the writing process onerous; features such as word prediction, tailor-made word banks and 'speech feedback' (hearing their work read back to them) enable them to produce a better piece of writing – something they can be proud of.

3 Teaching and learning

Our knowledge of how children learn and what normally are the characteristics of effective teaching have improved dramatically over the last few decades. Just like any other subject, RE lessons benefit from having a snappy start which makes pupils sit up and engages their attention. Being clear about the aim of the lesson and sharing that aim with the pupils can also greatly help. However, that does not mean launching into a lesson with a statement about the aim of the lesson on the whiteboard and requiring pupils to laboriously copy out the statement into their exercise books. When identifying an aim, it is usually better to avoid a statement which is very unspecific. Telling young people that the aim of the lesson is to deepen their understanding of the Bible might sound impressive but is likely to result in uncertainty as to whether that aim has been achieved. Whereas if the aim can be specified in a clearer form, for example 'By the end of the lesson you will know about three reasons which many Christians give for believing that the Bible is a holy book', pupils can leave a lesson with a clearer sense of achievement and knowing that they have gained something.

Plenaries are also an important weapon in the RE teacher's arsenal. They make it possible for pupils to demonstrate and reinforce what they have learnt. However, it is important that plenaries should involve the pupils so that it is pupils who are required to recall, explain, analyse or evaluate. That a plenary should involve pupils making the effort to recall or explain is vital, as it is this effort that will help pupils to gain and strengthen the synaptic link which is essential for the formation of memory. If instead a plenary is little more than the teacher telling the pupils what they have been taught, the chance that pupils will retain anything which can be built on later is much less likely.

There can be few people today involved in education who are not aware of Howard Gardner's ideas about multiple intelligences (Gardner 2011). Using his ideas in their simplest form, we know some young people in our classrooms respond well to visual input, some to auditory input, while others are mainly kinaesthetic learners. In order to establish an inclusive classroom the teacher of RE must respond to the learning strengths of different children and try to accommodate their different needs.

Visual stimuli

Most people find that learning something is easier if a picture is provided. For large numbers of young people with learning difficulties, a diet largely of words, whether spoken or written, unsupported by visual material seriously limits their ability to learn. However, a great amount of religious material is available to us visually. The following are just some examples of how to make effective use of visual material.

Deciphering visual information

It is important that the teacher of RE avoids being over-didactic by being the sole provider of an explanation or commentary on visual material that is under investigation. Instead, the teacher of RE should help pupils to develop their visual and oral skills by giving them opportunities to decipher information for themselves. For example, pupils might be provided with a photograph or perhaps a video clip which shows an infant baptism, or a Muslim undertaking obligatory worship, or a Jewish man putting on tefillin (phylacteries). The pupils should then be given several minutes looking and thinking time before being invited to report back on what they can see in the photograph or video or what they thought about the ceremony they have seen. Pupils should be encouraged to move beyond simply recalling information by being asked to suggest what might be the motive or reason behind why this ceremony or ritual is taking place, or what it means. Invite the pupils to consider – apart from what you can see – what is really going on.

Suggest motive and purpose

Children with learning difficulties don't want to be patronised with tasks which are too easy. To create more challenge, pupils might be asked to suggest what cannot be seen, that is, motive, purpose, feelings, or the expression or affirming of beliefs. Children again should be given several minutes to look and think before they answer. Questions should be phrased without fussy elaboration, for example 'Look at the photo – why do you think this man is doing this?' The teachers should try to avoid suggesting in their tone or manner that there is a single correct answer or that they know the answer and the child has to somehow guess what the teacher is thinking.

Storyboarding

Children with learning difficulties can find it easier to recall the details of a story using visual memory based on storyboarding. Teachers of RE do need to avoid becoming too preoccupied, or bogged down, with the accuracy with which children can recall a religious story. Religious stories such as the Easter story, the Genesis creation story or the Sikh Baisakhi story are important. However, being able to accurately recall them is of secondary importance compared with having an insight into what the story may be telling us, or how it may be widely understood by members of the faith for which the story is of special significance, or how the story may inform our own lives regardless of whether one has a religious faith or not. It can happen that children will repeatedly stumble over the details of a story, but just because they cannot get the recall exactly right does not mean that they should not be given an opportunity to respond to a story. A pupil who finds it difficult to articulate the details may still have a sufficiently effective grasp of the story and know it well enough in outline, so that they are capable of transcending the informative and talking about what the story means or why it may have particular religious significance.

Religious art

Visual images are not just neutral records of reality. This is particularly true of religious art. Pupils should be encouraged to look at religious art and ask questions such as 'What is the artist trying to say?' and 'What beliefs is the artist trying to express?' Children who may have difficulty with reading and writing can often show a shrewd ability to read an image.

In order to create an opportunity for pupils to do this, it is important to avoid the temptation to tell pupils what an image might mean. That's not to say pupils should be just left to their own devices. In RE it is clearly appropriate to draw pupils' attention to certain aspects of an image, to ask pertinent questions, to suggest clues or give hints in order to encourage pupils to think independently but also to think in a way which is both informed and coherent. Giving pupils looking and thinking time not only encourages them to become increasingly independent as thinkers, but it is also likely they will come up with ideas and answers which will stay with them long after they have forgotten anything that the teacher might have told them.

Comparing religious art

The claim that artists have beliefs and attitudes which are reflected in the art they produce can be made even clearer by comparing the work of two pieces of art. Particularly in Christian art, over the centuries, certain themes have been tackled by many artists. This makes it possible to directly compare the views represented in two works of art. For example, pupils might be invited to compare Grunewald's *Crucifixion, the Isenheim Altarpiece* with Raphael's painting of the same subject in the *Mond Crucifixion.* Pupils might be invited to consider questions such as those suggested below:

- What does this painting tell you?
- What are the two artists trying to say?
- Why does Raphael show both the sun and the moon in his painting?
- Does Christ look to be in agony in the painting?
- Why has Raphael painted Christ in this way?
- What are the angels in Raphael's painting doing?
- Why did Raphael include angels in his painting?
- How is Grunewald's image of Christ different from Raphael's?
- Why has Grunewald painted Christ in this way?
- What other differences or similarities can you see in the two paintings?
- What do you think these differences or similarities suggest?

Implicit religious images

Many children have little experience of organised religion. There are also plenty of children that view any organised authority as an irrelevance which does not understand or address their needs. And yet many of these young people are privately working on issues going on inside their head which are of a profoundly religious nature. It is for this reason that, when given the opportunity to pause and wonder at visual material like a rural landscape, moonlight on water or a close-up of a chrysanthemum, young people can astonish us with the quality of the questions these images pose for them.

As well as images of the natural world, images which remind us of the social and emotional world we live in can be equally stimulating. Some of these may reflect pain and grief in the world, for example a village destroyed by an earthquake, a victim of a brutal crime or the mushroom cloud of a hydrogen bomb. Some images have a message of hope and joy, for example the loving care of a trained nurse, the companionship and joy in the faces of an elderly married couple or the laughter of street children playing in a slum.

Objects and artefacts

Images which raise questions and stimulate healthy discussion do not have to be two-dimensional. Arranging the pupils into a circle and placing in the centre of the circle a single object, like an acorn, an expensive cosmetic, a vase of decaying flowers, a fashionable smartphone, a pair of designer-label trainers, can serve as a stimulus to lively discussion. Pupils who sometimes hardly ever speak are suddenly revealed as informed students of globalisation, the power of the media (including social media), materialism, spirituality, human happiness, death and decay. A religious artefact can similarly be used as a stimulus. A quality artefact, for example a Shiva Nata-raja, a crucifix or an image of a laughing Buddha, can provide the prompt for a discussion on what God is like, the purpose of prayer, the role of sacrifice and perhaps in what sense the word salvation might be used.

Figure 3.1 For maximum educational impact, do not simply display religious artefacts, but introduce them to pupils with a sense of drama and significance using a strategy known as 'controlled disclosure'.

© Fox Lane Photography

Controlled disclosure

It is important to try to add a sense of drama to the experience of first seeing an artefact. In RE this is commonly called 'controlled disclosure'. The object should be covered and so cannot be seen as the pupils take their seats. When the pupils are ready and their attention is focused, the cover is removed and the experience begins. Sometimes the disclosing of the object is made even more interesting by removing only part of the cover, or by allowing the students a partial experience of the artefact by letting them touch it underneath the cover but not see the object itself. The point of this is that the disclosure should not be casual but should have a sense of occasion or theatre about it. It is also important to present a religious artefact as far as is possible with a sense of quality and respect. After all, a religious artefact may often embody some of the most deeply felt convictions a human may have. To achieve this sense of respect it is desirable to make use of signals, and a quality stand, a tablecloth or a coloured velvet cover is often used. Children with learning difficulties are often sensitive to these signals. Certainly a religious artefact must not be presented in any way that could be perceived as being casual, sloppy or disrespectful in any way.

A single stimulus

The power of the strategy is not increased by using more and more images or artefacts. Showing young people many images of poverty can turn them off, making them immune or increasingly indifferent to human suffering and thereby impoverishing rather than heightening the experience. Showing many images or artefacts related to prayer may confuse the issue and raise too many questions. A single stimulus, such as a well-presented image or artefact which the pupils are given plenty of time to reflect on, can have a much more powerful impact.

Films and video

As well as the still image, the value of the moving image in the inclusive RE classroom should not be ignored. Using downloaded video, it is now possible to show pupils Buddhists engaged in meditation, Muslims undertaking the hajj, Christians receiving holy communion, Humanists talking about a non-religious funeral, Sikhs distributing food in the langar, Hindus bathing in the Ganges and Jews celebrating the Passover. Using child-friendly cartoon characters, Christian, Sikh, Hindu and Buddhist stories can be shown to young pupils with little more effort than pressing the 'play' button.

Given all this material, one would think the teacher of RE could hardly fail in the classroom. However, the video is not a passport to RE Shangri-La. Often RE video material is decidedly uninteresting for young people. A great deal of religious video material rarely has any lavish special effects, the pace is often drawn out and the language is frequently little more than a humourless, factual, descriptive commentary. There are, of course, some notable exceptions and a major source of quality video material which many teachers of RE make use of is True Tube (see www.truetube.co.uk/).

Nevertheless, a teacher would be unwise to imagine that, by simply inviting children to watch an RE video (whether commercially produced or freely available), they are assured of providing high-quality religious education. Because of the limitations of a good deal of the material available, it is often inappropriate to play the whole twenty or thirty minutes of an RE video. Many children tend to become mentally passive, or indeed bored, when watching video material for any length of time. Initial interest can quickly drain away and, because of this, it is often advisable to use video in short bursts of little more than two or three minutes, sometimes even less. Short clips of video material might be interspersed with comment, discussion, questioning and perhaps some analysis of what they have seen. It is often in the discussion of the video that the largest educational gain may be made. Video material often carries several different messages, so it can help if young people are invited to focus on one specific task prior to viewing. For example, it might be suggested to pupils, as they watch a video which shows the pilgrimage to Makkah, that they should try to identify two ways in which an individual might spiritually benefit from going on such a pilgrimage. An assignment of this kind is often avoided in favour of a task which invites pupils to gain factual information. A not untypical example of this is to ask pupils prior to watching a video to find answers to questions such as:

1. What is the name of the city the pilgrims travel to?
2. What is the building called that the pilgrims walk around?
3. How many times do the pilgrims walk around this building?
4. What is the proper name Muslims have for the pilgrimage?
5. What is the name given to the clothing pilgrims wear? etc.

Teaching 'facts', particularly things like the 'proper' word for an object or ceremony within a religious tradition, is frequently used in RE and a similar approach is often recommended by adherents of religious traditions. The thinking behind this is that factual information is often regarded as the proper starting point, the bedrock, which pupils need to know before moving on to deeper issues. Teaching 'facts' about religion is often an approach used by teachers because it is seen as safe; providing largely uncontested and uncontroversial information is unlikely to give rise to any criticism. However, becoming acquainted with factual information about religion, particularly the learning of religious terminology for rituals, objects, clothing, food, etc., is likely, at best, to make only a weak contribution to a child's religious education. Too much value is often placed on knowing whether a particular religious object or ceremony is called this or that. Such knowledge often has hardly any significance in the lives of many pupils; it connects to so little that is important to them that such knowledge is often not securely retained. Ask pupils seven or eight weeks after they have been taught about the 'hajj', the 'tawaf' or the 'ka'ba' what is the proper name Muslims have for the pilgrimage or what is the name of the building pilgrims walk around and many will have difficulties providing a correct answer. Poor learning in RE is often associated with what is being taught and whether it has any connection, significance or meaning in children's lives.

The real purpose of teaching RE strives for something much deeper. The experience which many Muslims have while on pilgrimage is that it brings together fellow Muslims from all corners of the world. Another feature of the pilgrimage is that it is physically demanding and that the shared experience of effort and exertion encourages a sense of camaraderie amongst pilgrims. Individuals often bond together so much that they come to a much deeper realisation of a truth half-known but not experienced intensely, in a way which takes on meaning for them. That truth is that nationality, race, class, colour and many other things that put barriers between people are fundamentally irrelevant compared to those things which humans have in common. After undertaking the pilgrimage, many Muslims talk about the experience of being a member of one humanity created by one God and that often that experience stays with them for the rest of their lives. Pupils should develop an understanding about all of this in RE and so gain a deeper insight into what the hajj might mean, and be able to use it as a chance to reflect upon their own attitudes to people around them, if we do not facilitate this, we are wasting an important opportunity.

Video can be turned into a far less passive medium if young people are entrusted with a camcorder and invited to make their own video. Some teachers have had tremendous success with young people who have found it very difficult to learn in the classroom but have recorded thoughtful comments on camera, reflecting on what it is like, for example, to be a young Muslim growing up in Britain or a young atheist explaining the reasons why they find it untenable that there is a compassionate God.

Contemporary film

Contemporary film can often provide rich material which the teacher of RE can make use of. Some films have a fairly obvious religious content, for example Richard Attenborough's *Gandhi*, Franco Zeffirelli's *Jesus of Nazareth*, Moustapha Akkad's *The Message*, Michael Aptect's *Amazing Grace*, Stephen Frears' *Philomena,* Ridley Scott's *Exodus: Gods and Kings,* Darren Aronofsky's *Noah* and Tom McCarthy's *Spotlight.* But sometimes films draw upon and explore spiritual and religious themes in a far less explicit way. Judicious use of this material can help students to recognise in popular youth culture a depth which they have sensed themselves but may not have fully appreciated. *The Matrix*, for example, provides a classic example of how, along with lots of action and violence, a film may also be a medium for exploring issues like the power of illusion, the idea that goes back to Plato that the reality we know is an illusion and that there may be a transcendent other world which is our real home and dwelling place. *Star Wars* and *Lord of the Rings* present spectacular accounts of good against evil set in the form of classic dualism. *Lord of the Rings* also offers an interesting perspective on the danger of power and who should wield it. *Terminator 2* raises significant questions about the sanctity of life, the difference between man and machine, and how sacrifice may be needed if salvation is to be achieved. The film *I, Robot* similarly gives rise to profound questions as to whether there is a difference between human and machine: can a machine ever make a moral decision? Can it ever be guilty, or feel guilt, or envy, or any emotion? Can a machine determine its own purpose or destiny or give its existence meaning? *Toy Story* has a lot to say about rivalry, fear of the newcomer, loyalty and courage. *The Hunger Games* illustrates how being heroic may be unintended and unassuming, while the film also has some pointedly critical things to say about hedonism, fashion, economic inequality and violence as entertainment. *Wild* tells the story not just of a physical journey but also of the spiritual journey of a young woman who is trying to find herself.

Soaps and series

It is well known that TV soaps have over the years featured major storylines on moral and social issues, such as euthanasia, adultery, domestic violence, racism and abortion. However, it is also true that a number of cult TV series have survived because they contain a great deal of thoughtful writing. *Star Trek*, for example, explores themes (often with subtlety) such as diversity, what it means to be human, how under stress the human spirit can grow, and the aspiration to strive and make more of oneself (see www.watch-episodes.com/star-trek-the-next-generation). In among the jokes, *The Simpsons* has all sorts of references to religion and theology, like Bart selling his soul, Homer breaking the eighth commandment and Lisa as the voice of Christian social awareness.

This material opens up real possibilities in the RE classroom for young people who have learning difficulties. Pupils who may have very little to say about Divali or Confirmation or kosher food may have a great deal to say of a religious nature about something that is included in a film or a TV programme they know well and feel passionate about.

Auditory stimuli

Some people have a particularly strong response to sound. They find that their ability to learn is much improved if the learning environment is aurally enriched.

Religious music

The strong association between music and particular religions can be used to establish a memorable theme. So, for example, as the pupils enter a classroom, have playing the song 'To Life' from *Fiddler on the Roof*. This can set the theme of the lesson, which is about the gusty joy and exuberant way in which many Jewish festivals like Purim and Simchat Torah are celebrated. The sound of the harmonium and tabla may be used to mark the beginning of a lesson about Sikh worship.

We know that our minds are alerted and that we pay much more attention if things happen that are out of the ordinary. Being attentive to things in our environment that are different or unusual has evolved as a survival technique. The more we can make lessons exceptional or different and take children by surprise, for example with the shock of the London Community Gospel Choir ringing in their ears, the greater are the chances that learning will take place.

Mood music

Music may also be used which has no particular religious associations, but which may set the appropriate mood in order to reinforce the lesson. For example, a group of pupils report to the whole class the story of Dietrich Bonhoeffer and his resistance to the Nazis; as they do so, Carl Davis's theme for *The World at War* is played in the background. As the pupils tell the story, there is an intensity in the classroom which, had there been no music, would have been absent.

Contemporary music

Contemporary rock and pop music is very important in the lives of many young people. Although much of it may have little substance, some of the best provides a genuine mini-commentary on serious issues which morally, spiritually and religiously are highly relevant. For example, Pink in 'Family Portrait' assumes the voice of a young girl experiencing the break-up of her parents' marriage. Shania Twain in 'Ka-Ching' mocks a world which makes a religion of having commodities. The Black Eyed Peas in 'Where Is the Love?' deplores negative images which contaminate the minds of young people and asks what has happened to the values of humanity? Chris Rea in 'Tell Me There's a Heaven' sings about how the belief in heaven may be a source, perhaps a necessary source, of comfort and consolation. Van Morrison in 'Full Force Gale' gives voice to how his faith lifts him up and provides for him a sanctuary from the setbacks that we all experience. Iris DeMent in 'He Reached Down' draws attention to core aspects of Jesus' teaching and perhaps more than hints at the idea of Incarnation. Tim Minchin as an atheist identifies in 'White Wine in the Sun' his serious reservations about and distaste for religion, while acknowledging that the coming together of families at Christmas has a quality about it which is undoubtedly appealing.

The potential of this material in the RE classroom for drawing young people into thought and discussion is immense. However, using contemporary music in RE is fraught with danger and has to be handled carefully. It is important that the teacher doesn't come across as false, attempting to exploit the popularity of youth culture.

Combining music with images

Contemporary music can be very effectively combined with visual images which provide a springboard to reflection and discussion. Young people, perhaps working with a partner, could be invited to select a piece of music which they feel has something significant to say. Their task is to combine the music with some still images. Before beginning the task, a discussion with the pupils takes place so that there is agreement about the sort of messages and values that would be appropriate. After the teacher has had a chance to preview the work, the finished product could be shown to the other pupils. The possibilities of drawing upon young people's strengths using ICT with this sort of assignment are clear.

Reflection time

RE has an important role in educating young people's emotions and feelings. One important way of achieving this is by building in reflection time. For example, in a lesson about Martin Luther King, using improvised drama, the pupils explore situations involving racism. In the discussion that follows, a pupil describes their own recent experience of racism. There is a genuine sense of outrage at the injustice. The teacher suggests that they should have time for reflection. A candle is lit and the teacher invites the pupils to think about what it is like to be the victim of racism and what they can do to stop racism. There is silence in the room for over a minute. Following the reflection time, the teacher invites pupils to share, if they wish, what thoughts they had while they were reflecting. A number of the pupils describe their feelings about racism and suggest ways of combating it.

However, reflection time cannot just be inserted into an RE lesson at any arbitrary point; the teacher has to plan a lesson so that the reflection time is appropriate.

Reflection time and music

It is, however, true that some young people find it difficult to cope with silence and stillness. For those pupils who are initially restless, this usually disappears over a short period of time as they get used to the experience. Reflection time can be supported by the use of music, usually slow and restful. Music which has a mystical quality can be particularly helpful, as found in the pan flute music of Gheorghe Zamfir or in pieces like Erik Satie's *Gymnopédies.*

Guided fantasy

Another way of supporting reflection time is by the use of guided fantasy. Guided fantasy is when the teacher, usually working from a prepared script, invites the pupils to imagine situations in which reflection or relaxation may be made easier. The teacher may begin by saying, for example, 'Imagine you are leaving the classroom. It is a hot, sunny day. You are walking down a country lane and then you find yourself in a meadow . . .' As with reflection time, guided fantasy can also be supported by music.

Special effects

Although not specific to RE, there are certain sound effects and special clips of music which have widespread appeal for young people and support their learning. The ticking clock sound-effect from the TV programme *Countdown* can be played to mark the end of time available to pupils to complete a particular activity. There are plenty of other special sound-effects which alert pupils, generate interest, give lessons a touch of humour and make lessons more memorable; for example, *Mission Impossible* might accompany the story of Jackie Pullinger, and *Thus Spake Zarathustra* could herald a presentation on Creation.

Religious sounds

Just as there are certain three-dimensional religious artefacts, so there are also certain sounds which are associated with particular religious traditions. Examples of these include the sound of the Jewish Shofar or ram's horn, the Islamic call to prayer and Buddhist chanting; such sounds obviously do have a place in the RE classroom. However, as with three-dimensional artefacts, these sound artefacts have to be handled with care. The Islamic call to prayer, the adhan, for example, may have a haunting beauty when heard over the rooftops of Ankara. But the sound of a recording played through a couple of two-watt speakers can be very disappointing. If good recordings of such sounds cannot be found, a short discussion may be necessary so that pupils don't end up making inappropriate judgements.

Kinaesthetic approaches

We have become increasingly aware that asking pupils to stand up and do things is by far the most effective way to promote learning. The following are some examples of kinaesthetic strategies which can be applied in the RE classroom.

Religious artefacts

Bringing physical objects such as a Qur'an, a chalice or a menorah into the classroom makes a religion much more real to young people. Appropriate respect has to be accorded to these objects in their presentation and handling. Pupils can gain a much more memorable encounter if they are permitted to have a hands-on experience. The appropriate handling of religious artefacts, picking up the signals from the teacher, is part of the lesson in respect which these objects make possible.

Providing a contrast

One way of varying the experience and of highlighting the special features of an artefact is by contrasting a religious artefact with a non-religious object. Pupils might, for example, be invited to identify the difference between the uncomfortable, prickly feel of a coconut doormat compared with the soft, velvety feel of a Muslim prayer mat. The contrasting difference in the colour, with prayer mats often being produced in luxurious emerald and turquoise, might also be noted. The rich velvety feel and the luxurious colours convey the idea that prayer in Islam is regarded as being something which is of great spiritual value to the individual. Obligatory prayer in Islam is understood as a gift which comes from God. It is not undertaken as if it is a duty or a chore to be got out of the way.

Simulation or mock ritual

Religious ceremonies and festivals like infant baptism, the Passover meal, Arti and Amrit particularly lend themselves to simulation. It is important to make it clear that what is taking place is not a real baptism or a real arti. Real religious ceremonies and rituals involve the inner intentions and beliefs of the participants. A simulation is an attempt to reconstruct the external movements and words of a religious ritual. Only volunteers should be asked to take part, and frequently it is well worthwhile for the teacher to freeze the action and remind all present that what is happening is not a real religious ceremony but a simulation. Special touches which can add to the reality of the simulation are also well worthwhile. So a simulated Passover meal is much more memorable if the pupils get to eat some genuine matzah (unleavened bread) and some prepared haroset.

The visit

As an opportunity for an experience which provides pupils with a lasting memory, the RE visit has few rivals. Although it involves a large investment of time, the rewards can be tremendous. The great majority of RE visits are to places of worship – for example, churches, mosques, gurdwaras – but other possibilities include exhibitions like the Beth Shalom Holocaust Centre, the IPCI Exhibition on Islam and the Anne Frank Exhibition.

Visits often have an unexpected educational bonus. Young people, for example, are often impressed by the generosity of members of the Sikh community or the friendliness they experience in the mosque. Visits often remove the sense of wariness and distrust or may counter stereotypes that pupils may have acquired from the media. They often result in improved relationships between teachers and pupils as the pupils are conscious that the teacher has made an effort on their behalf.

Figure 3.2 A visit to a place of worship can have an unexpected educational bonus.
© Fox Lane Photography

Although there are usually spin-off benefits to visits, it is still advisable to plan so that there is a clear learning objective. Establishing a good first-hand contact with the member of the faith community that will greet your party and show them around can be of great help. A visit is usually of much more benefit if the pupils are given clear opportunities to meet members of the faith community, focus on significant features of the building and ask questions which have been considered prior to the visit. Children with learning difficulties can often be helped to get something extra out of a visit by giving them a special task or activity. For example, they might be given charge of a digital camera or video camcorder to make a photographic record of their visit, or use a digital audio recorder to make an audio diary of their visit.

The natural world

A very valuable resource for the teacher of RE is the natural world outside the classroom. Children can learn a great deal through activities like 'Hoop', 'Trust walk' or 'Sounds'. 'Hoop' involves taking pupils to a field or patch of grass on a dry day. The pupils put a hoop on the ground and spend some time carefully looking at what can be seen inside the hoop. After a while the pupils come together and share their discoveries and thoughts. 'Trust walk' has the pupils working together in pairs. One pupil is the leader and the other pupil is blindfolded. In a natural area, the leader guides their partner, visiting smells, shapes and textures. 'Sounds' involves having the pupils lie down on their backs with both fists held up in the air. Whenever they hear a sound, which may be a leaf falling, the wind in the trees or a bird singing, the pupil lifts a finger. After a while the pupils are invited to reflect and then talk about the experience.

Activities like these may be criticised because they provide little in the way of overt learning about religion. This would be a fair criticism if the pupils were only invited to stare at a patch of grass for a while and nothing else. The reflection and sharing of responses are essential. The purpose of these activities is to bring young people closer to the original experiences which probably gave rise to religious impulses in the first place. By doing so, pupils may gain a much greater understanding of the questions and feelings which form the basis of religious faith.

'Human bar chart'

'Human bar chart' enables self-conscious adolescents to have their view on an issue expressed without having to reveal their own position. Pupils are invited to think about an issue, such as 'Does prayer really work?' After some thinking time, the pupils record their attitude by choosing a number 1 to 5 which they write on a piece of paper (see Appendix 13). Number 1 represents the view that there is a very low chance that prayer works. Number 5 represents the view that there is a very high chance. The paper with the number on it is left unsigned and placed in a box. After the papers have been jumbled up, each pupil removes a paper from the box. Numbers 1 to 5 are placed on the floor. The pupils are invited to form a human bar chart by standing in line by the number on the floor which corresponds to the number they picked out of the box. Seeing how the views of the class vary, the pupils might be invited to suggest reasons why people hold different views on this issue. Or in some cases pupils, realising they are not alone in their views, feel encouraged to talk about their beliefs.

'Human continuum'

'Human continuum' involves inviting the pupils to imagine a line in the classroom. One end of the line represents a point of view. The other end represents the opposite point of view. The space between the two ends represents the various shades of grey. Following discussion on a controversial issue, for example 'Has religion been more responsible for peace than war?', pupils are asked to stand in the space on the continuum line which most accurately represents their view.

Pupils are often surprised by the position taken up by fellow classmates, and this can prompt deeper discussion. Another advantage of the technique for the inclusive classroom is that it enables all pupils to say where they stand on an issue, even though articulating their view neatly into words might be difficult for them.

Role-play

There is a whole range of educational drama techniques like 'hot-seating', 'freeze frame' or 'robe of the expert' which lend themselves to adaptation in the RE classroom. Role-play usually involves improvised drama: two or three pupils are given a role and a scenario and are invited to role-play what might be said or done. A sample scenario is included below.

Role-play scenario

In a school where most children are Christian or nominally Christian, Sikh pupils are being mocked for wearing the turban.

> **Role 1**: Kimberley thinks what is going on in the school is a harmless bit of fun and that Sikhs in the school shouldn't be so sensitive.

> **Role 2**: Darren thinks that all Christians have a responsibility to stop racial and religious intolerance wherever they see it.

Role-play a scene between Kimberley and Darren where they explain their thinking and perhaps try to influence each other's opinions.

The role-play may be extended with additional pupils in role being invited to join the conversation:

> **Role 3**: Lisa thinks all signs of religious commitment should be banned in a school.

For successful improvised role-play, pupils do need to have some thinking and preparation time. They should also be given an opportunity to step out of role and talk about how they felt about the role.

Mime

Some children, when asked to describe a baptism or how Muslims worship, shrug their shoulders or look blank, apparently in complete ignorance of such rituals. In some cases, such a response does not necessarily mean that they do not have any knowledge of such rituals. Mime can help children show that they have a body memory of rituals, ceremonies and festivals which is not easily available to them in language. The pupils are given some planning or research time. They then mime the ritual. The rest of the pupils, perhaps provided with a list of choices, guess what ritual is being mimed.

4 Monitoring and assessment

For over two decades a system using eight levels has dominated our assessment in national curriculum subjects in England and Wales. The intention was that each 'level' described a step up in difficulty so that a parent, teacher or indeed anyone interested would know that a pupil who had attained level 2 in a subject would be working at a higher level than a child who had attained a level 1, and so on. The system had an appealing simplicity. The belief was that it would introduce more objectivity and accountability into education. Having a common set of levels, it was claimed, would make it possible to compare all schools across the country, north and south, east and west. It was hoped levels would introduce a more rigorous system that would make it possible to identify those schools and subject departments in schools which were more effective and which regularly helped pupils to achieve higher educational standards, as well as less effective schools which consistently failed to do this.

Levels in RE

Religious education, however, has never been a part of the national curriculum; instead its content is determined locally. It follows then that, subject to certain limits, it is up to each local authority to decide on how assessment should be undertaken in locally controlled community schools and voluntary controlled schools.

Information about what a school should do when it comes to assessment in RE is usually provided in the local authority's RE agreed syllabus, with varying degrees of helpfulness.

The 2004 NFRE RE levels

In 2004, in an attempt to establish standards and provide a means by which assessment in RE could improve, the DfES and the QCA published 'The Non-statutory National Framework for Religious Education' (NFRE). This document (DfE 2004) built upon an earlier advisory document (QCA 2000) by providing an eight-level scale plus an Exceptional Performance level. Each level on this scale is expressed in the form of two attainment targets, so, for each level, part of the statement refers to 'Attainment target 1: Learning about religion', while the other part refers to 'Attainment target 2: Learning from religion'. Although these levels had no statutory status, perhaps because they had the authority of the QCA and in general the support of faith communities, they were very well received. They were widely adopted by local authorities and they continue to be used in a large number of RE agreed syllabuses, where sometimes they are slightly amended for better clarification.

Pupil speak and can-do-statements

Alongside the NFRE levels, some RE agreed syllabuses provide a non-technical 'pupil speak' version of the same levels. These are written in fairly simple language in the hope that most pupils will be able to understand them. Other agreed syllabuses provided 'can-do-statements' which are similarly written in non-technical language. The attempts to express levels in more straight-forward language make it more likely pupils will know what they have to do to improve in RE. This approach also facilitates self-assessment and peer assessment in the subject.

Often the 'can-do-statements' that are published in agreed syllabuses are either copies of or slightly amended versions of those available on the RE Online website (see www.reonline.org.uk/assessing/how/can-do-statements/). These statements also make use of the two attainment targets 'AT 1 Learning about religion' and 'AT 2 Learning from religion'. Each 'can-do-statement' refers to six 'Strands' or 'Areas of Enquiry'; broadly speaking, the first three (1–3) of these apply to 'AT1 Learning about religion' and the last three (4–6) apply to 'AT2 Learning from religion'.

P scales

Some agreed syllabuses also provide 'performance descriptors' or 'P scales' or 'P levels' (see Appendix 4). P scales are non-statutory guidelines for assessing the performance of pupils aged 5–16 with special educational needs and disabilities who cannot access the national curriculum. The DfE (2014) makes P scales available for all national curriculum subjects in a document called 'Performance – P Scale – Attainment Targets for Pupils with Special Educational Needs' (July 2014; see www.gov.uk/government/publications/p-scales-attainment-targets-for-pupils-with-sen). P scales for religious education are included in the document as an annex. Scales P1 to P3 are the same for all curriculum subjects, but P4 to P8 are subject specific. The religious education P7 and P8 statements resemble in certain respects level 1 and level 2 in the NFRE 2004 levels. For example:

Religious education P scales (July 2014)		NFRE Religious education levels (2004)	
P7	They may communicate their feelings about what is special to them	Level 1	Pupils talk about their own experiences and feelings . . .
P8	They begin to understand that religious and other stories carry moral and religious meaning	Level 2	Pupils retell religious stories and suggest meanings for actions and symbols

Levels and voluntary-aided schools

Many Church of England voluntary-aided schools which do not have to teach RE in accordance with the locally agreed syllabus do in fact do so. Catholic voluntary-aided schools, however, do not in most cases make use of the local LA agreed syllabus. Instead, the RE in these schools is determined by each diocesan board of education or, perhaps to be more correct, by each diocesan bishop. The Catholic Education Service in 2006 published a booklet called *Levels of Attainment in Religious Education in Catholic Schools and Colleges* (see http://edurcdhn.org.uk/downloads/oldkeep/secmarch2010/Attainment%20Levels.pdf). This booklet contains a set of RE 'Levels of Attainment' from level 1 to level 8 and also an Exceptional Performance level. These levels are not identical to, but do bear some resemblance to, the 2004 NFRE levels in that the two attainment targets 'Learning about religion' and 'Learning from religion' are used and the wording of some of the level descriptors is very similar. The booklet also contains exemplification material and also P scales which are identical to the DfE P scales.

The case against levels

Although the hope was that the 2004 NFRE levels would provide a common benchmark for determining standards in RE and would improve the quality of assessment in RE, there is little evidence to suggest that they have in fact done so. In Ofsted reports on RE which were published in 2007, 2010 and 2013, Ofsted inspectors were unable to find any evidence that assessment in RE was improving or that standards of attainment were rising. For example, in 2010, six years after the NFRE levels had been published, an Ofsted report called *Transforming Religious Education* claimed that, in both 'the primary and the secondary phases, most teachers were experiencing significant difficulties in using the levels of attainment set out in the locally agreed syllabus'. The report went on to say that, in 'most of the schools visited, judgements about pupils' progress made using levels were very inaccurate'. The report also said that data available to subject leaders was 'too unreliable to provide an effective basis for self-evaluation'.

The 2013 Ofsted report *Religious Education: Realising the Potential* claimed that, in seven out of ten secondary schools inspected, assessment in RE was 'less than good' and in nearly one in five secondary schools it was judged to be 'inadequate'. Assessment in religious education was particularly ineffective, but the quality of assessment in other subjects was also not good.

The National Curriculum Expert Panel report

In December 2011 the National Curriculum Expert Panel published its report *The Framework for the National Curriculum*. The members of the Expert Panel concluded that assessment based on levels was not effective. This was thought to be particularly true for children with SEN and disabilities. Assessment, the report claimed, should not be based on 'abstracted and arbitrary expressions of the curriculum', which is what levels offered. Levels had led to pupils labelling themselves in terms of their level and being more concerned about what level they were at rather than the 'substance of what they know, can do and understand'.

The report maintained that assessment for all children, but particularly for children with SEND, 'should focus on successes rather than being grounded in failure'. Being labelled as 'level 2' or 'level 3' in a class where most pupils were a 'level 4' only served to undermine children and remind them of their failure.

The most serious problem with using levels, the report maintained, was that it led to a system which lacked 'curriculum coherence'. This referred to the idea that there was no coherent close relationship between the curriculum content that was being taught and the levels that were being used for assessment. This resulted in well-intentioned teachers interpreting them in many different ways. The claim that levels provided a sort of yardstick which could be used to compare one child against another, wherever they were being taught in the country, simply was not true as teachers in different parts of the country, indeed even in the same school, were interpreting the levels differently. Fundamentally the levels lacked validity.

Levels and validity

The criticism that the levels were non-specific, abstract statements which led to different teachers interpreting them differently described a problem many felt was true of the RE levels. For example, the NFRE level 3 statement tells us that pupils should be able to 'make links between beliefs and sources, including religious stories and sacred texts'. But what exactly do these words mean?

What sort of links between stories and beliefs does this level descriptor refer to? A concrete example will help illustrate the problem. Imagine a situation in which children were taught about a religious story, for example the story of Jesus ~~stilling the~~ storm (Mt 8 v. 23–27, Mk 4 v. 35–41, Lk v. 22–25). In the course of a series of lessons the pupils are asked, 'What does the story tell us about Jesus or what people believe about him?' The exercise might result in a variety of different answers but three typical responses that pupils might give are:

> *Ellie's response*: 'People believe Jesus was a nice man because he cared about the disciples in the boat.'
> *Liam's response*: 'People believe Jesus could perform miracles.'
> *Helen's response*: 'People believe Jesus was the Son of God so when he told the wind and waves to 'Be still' the wind and the waves did what he said because he was the Son of God.'

All three of these responses, on the face of it, seem to meet the level 3 requirement. Does this mean that the evidence so far suggests all three pupils are working at the same level of attainment? Are all three pupils achieving a level 3? Or is the level statement so vague and non-specific that when applied in real circumstances the statement is of little help as it fails to distinguish low from higher attaining pupils? With these questions in mind, it is worthwhile examining the three responses in detail.

Ellie's response

It might vary depending on who one asked, but many would think that Ellie's answer is the least satisfactory response. Ellie's response is not wrong but it falls rather short of being an adequate answer. Ellie claims that the story suggests that Jesus cared about his disciples. This answer is true; however, the story reveals something about the nature of Jesus which is much deeper and of much greater religious or theological significance which Ellie has failed to recognise. Ellie's response lacks what might be called theological insight or depth. Her ability to only see a moral but not a religious dimension to the story reveals a lack of religious literacy. Technically, Ellie may have delivered on what is expressed in the level 3 statement – after all, she is able to make a link between a religious story and a belief. However, given this particular religious story, Ellie's focus on the moral dimension is a very simple and obvious one, and it falls short of the response one might expect for a child of her age.

Liam's response

Unlike Ellie's answer, Liam's response could be said to show some theological awareness. However, his answer is still of a fairly simple kind. Liam understands the story reveals Jesus as a man who could perform a miracle. However, his answer does not go on to make it clear that the word 'miracle' is usually associated with an event that God is involved in some sense in bringing about. In other words, an event is usually only considered to be genuinely a miracle if it has divine agency. Liam is right to focus on the miracle that is described in this story as being of greater significance than any moral message it might have, and it is this awareness that makes his answer better than Ellie's. However, Liam doesn't go on to make the connection that performing a miracle suggests that Jesus is in some way helped by or connected or related to God or that perhaps God views Jesus in a special way different from other people. Like Ellie, Liam has delivered on what is expressed in the level 3 statement – he is able to make a link between a religious story and a belief. However, Liam's link is more theologically significant and is a great deal more relevant to the story than the link that Ellie was able to identify.

Helen's response

Helen's response is another step up again on Liam's answer. It shows that she understands that the story suggests that Jesus could perform miracles, but also that Jesus has a special relationship with God and that God also viewed Jesus in a special way, different from other people. Christians have traditionally expressed this special relationship by using the phrase the 'Son of God'. Helen correctly uses the phrase 'Son of God' in her answer and does so in a way which suggests that the story of Jesus stilling the storm is evidence that he is more than just a good man, or a miracle worker; Jesus has a special status or intimacy with God without which the miracle would not have been possible. Like Ellie and Liam, Helen has also delivered on what is expressed in the level 3 statement – she is able to make a link between a religious story and a belief. However, Helen's answer is of a higher order than that of either Ellie or Liam. Like Liam, Helen is aware that the story's real significance has to do with the miracle described in the story rather than any moral lessons to do with caring. Helen's insight into the story is greater than Liam's because she recognises that the story links to the belief that Jesus has a special and intimate relationship with God. Neither Ellie nor Liam are close to making this sort of link or showing an understanding of the story with this level of sophistication, but Helen is at least in part on the way.

The NFRE RE levels abound in problems of this kind. Many of the levels contain statements which are so general and non-specific that they can be thought to apply to pupils that have a very basic level of knowledge or understanding but equally they could be thought to apply to pupils that are showing a much higher level of attainment. This makes them vulnerable to conscientious teachers applying an interpretation which is very different from that of their equally conscientious colleagues.

Assessment without levels

In June 2012 Secretary of State Michael Gove responded to the report by the National Curriculum Expert Panel by agreeing that the current system of 'levels' should be removed. The new policy of the DfE was to desist from prescribing a detailed approach to assessment, as it was thought this did not 'fit with the curriculum freedoms we are giving schools'. Instead, schools were encouraged to develop their own approaches to formative assessment. The advice was limited to the suggestion that the assessment framework should be built into the school curriculum. The statement also made it clear that schools should be able to check what pupils have learnt and should know whether pupils are on track to meet end-of-Key-Stage expectations so that they can report regularly to parents.

The REC 'Review'

The response of the RE community to this new policy has been mixed. In October 2013 the Religious Education Council (REC) published a document called 'A Review of Religious Education in England', in parallel to the new national curriculum. The 'Review', as it is more usually referred to, was intended to succeed the QCA's 'Non-statutory National Framework for RE' (2004). It provides a discussion on assessment in RE (Appendix Two and a couple of preceding pages) and a 'progression grid' which contains statements about what pupils will be able to do at the end of Key Stage 1, 2 and 3. However, the 'progression grid' makes use of non-specific, generic statements, e.g. 'Retell and suggest meanings to some religious and moral stories . . .' and 'Explore and describe a range of beliefs, symbols and actions so they can understand different ways of life . . .', which makes them look vulnerable to the same problems experienced when using levels.

Summative assessment

Some schools and some SACREs (Standing Advisory Councils for Religious Education) have recognised that for assessment to improve in RE there needs to be a departure from steps, ladders and end-of-Key-Stage statements which use non-specific, generic statements. There is a need for a much more radical change in the culture of assessment away from the prominence that has been given for several decades to summative assessment. Summative assessment doesn't confront the real challenge, as it doesn't provide any clear information about why a child may not be making good progress or indeed why a child may be doing exceptionally well. This is especially true in the case of a child who has special educational needs and who may need advice and support of a very particular kind. To tackle that challenge one needs to know why a child may not be doing as well as they might and to know that quality formative assessment is needed.

Formative assessment

Quality formative assessment is about entering into a dialogue with pupils in order to provide useful feedback in language which pupils can understand so they know what to do to improve. This involves examining carefully what a child might write, say or do, in order to work out in what sense they are showing understanding or where exactly there might be gaps in their knowledge. It is about scrutinising their responses, trying to work out if they have really understood and, if not, what can be done to help them understand properly, or more accurately or more deeply. Sometimes formative assessment can be diagnostic; for example, a teacher might identify a particular misunderstanding or gap in a child's knowledge which, if it can be resolved, clears the way for that child to move forward. High-quality formative assessment often involves listening to pupils, talking the matter over with them and refining one's responses to help them move towards a deeper level of understanding or awareness.

Formative assessment is also about scrutinising oneself as a teacher. This is often called reflective teaching and involves judging one's own effectiveness in the classroom. It is about analysing how something was taught and asking oneself: 'Did I explain that idea well, could I have explained it better, is there a better approach or method I could have used?' Reflective teaching, of course, also involves acting on one's reflection and modifying one's teaching, or returning to a topic with the pupils in order to ensure that they properly understand and that they do really 'get it'.

Marking is a crucial part of formative assessment. All too often the view is expressed that there are no wrong answers in RE and so, not infrequently, marking of work in RE is little more than providing encouraging comments – like 'Well done – you have expressed your own view' – or vague exhortations to strive for more insight – 'Try to say more' or 'You need to think more deeply'. Marking has to be manageable of course and all work cannot be marked in great detail. Depending on other commitments and how many pupils a teacher might be responsible for, a fair amount of marking may involve 'Acknowledgment marking'. This is light-touch marking where the teacher largely checks that the work has been completed and there are no obvious mistakes. But some marking must be 'Quality teacher marking' which is formative marking designed to help pupils to know and understand what to do to improve. Levels or grades may accompany the comments as leadership in the school may require it for summative assessment purposes, but the main thrust of the marking should be to give pupils direction so they understand how they can improve.

With preparation, some work in RE can be appropriately marked using 'peer marking' and 'self-assessment marking'. This is not just a way of cutting down on the marking workload; peer and self-assessment marking can offer real advantages. It can deepen pupils' understanding of what the real aims of RE are, it can make them think more seriously about their own work, and it can also encourage a greater sense of maturity and responsibility, knowing that their judgement can be respected. If this process is modelled to the class (e.g. by using a visualiser), it can be highly effective in developing pupils' understanding of 'what a good one looks like' (WAGOLL). This activity also promotes discussion about assessment criteria and how pupils can demonstrate what they know and understand.

Not all formative marking requires a written statement. Religious education touches on sensitive and deeply complex issues. Sometimes feedback is not about straightforward advice or instruction. Often it is far more appropriate to discuss the matter with the child and to provide verbal feedback that is informed by that dialogue. 'Verbal feedback' stamps (with the ink contained within the stamper so no ink pad is needed) are easily available and can be a valuable marking aid for all teachers involved in RE. It can also be helpful to ask a pupil to write a brief summary of the verbal advice provided, alongside the stamp in their exercise book or on the relevant page in their work folder. This can ensure that the child has understood what was discussed and also make it less likely that the advice might be ignored or forgotten.

Core knowledge

The international evidence is that countries that have the most successful education systems take assessment very seriously but do not use levels. What they do is ensure that there is a close relationship between the content that is taught and the assessment that is undertaken. To achieve this, they specify for each subject the core knowledge that every child should be taught and should securely know.

A core knowledge curriculum is progressive and avoids repetition, but each stage of the programme makes children ready for the next stage so that it encourages not simply more secure learning but also greater depth of learning. There is certainly a concern that pupils should learn 'facts'; however, it is vital that they develop knowledge in a much deeper sense and this includes key concepts, beliefs, narratives, processes, language, ideas and skills.

Mastery

'Mastery' is an important idea associated with a core knowledge curriculum. This doesn't mean achieving an exceptionally high level of retention and understanding of the 'core knowledge', which only a small number of children would be expected to achieve. Rather, 'mastery' means breaking a subject down into discrete stages which have to be taught in a particular order with the expectation that all learners should have that secure knowledge before they can move on to the next stage. By mastering a stage, pupils are made 'stage ready' for what is next in the core knowledge curriculum. It may take some pupils longer to master a stage and they may need special support, but the expectation is that all will get there. No child is left behind or pushed on to the next stage if they are not yet ready. The likely outcome of such a policy is easily predictable. Expecting a child to learn new content for which they are not ready will almost inevitably lead to failure. They are likely to become demoralised and simply fall further behind, making the chances that they will ever catch up highly remote.

Core knowledge and RE

A main requirement to helping pupils who have SEND is to provide high-quality teaching that identifies and addresses their areas of weakness. For this reason, effective assessment must be capable of identifying where pupils may be experiencing difficulties or where knowledge and understanding may be weak. The way forward is likely to involve assessment which is more closely related to the content taught, as might be identified in an RE core knowledge curriculum which describes the content of what should be taught in much clearer, more specific terms than has been the case in the past. This is likely to be welcomed by teachers, especially those who have little specialist training in the subject.

However, although there are some local authorities that are giving serious consideration to the matter at the time of going to print, none have published an RE agreed syllabus which has a core knowledge curriculum or has a system of assessment which relates closely to the content. What should be in an RE core curriculum is a significant point of contention. It may be possible to specify an RE core curriculum that should be taught in a school where the majority of pupils are Christian and there are small numbers of pupils who are Sikh, Muslim and Hindu. However, it is unlikely that the teaching of that same core curriculum would be appropriate in another school which had a very large majority of Muslim pupils and just a handful of Christian pupils or pupils of no particular faith. Two schools of this kind might be less than half a mile from each other. Similarly, there are schools which have a large majority of Sikh pupils, while other schools have a substantial number of pupils that have little or no engagement with religion of any kind. The diversity of schools which have a very different religious or non-religious complexion when it comes to the pupils' backgrounds is enormous. For this reason it is very difficult to see how an RE core curriculum could be devised which would be suitable for all schools nationally or even for all schools in a local authority area.

The usual solution to this problem is to fudge the issue by describing what should be taught in RE in vague terms that everyone can agree as there is nothing to disagree about. The REC's 'Review' (2013), for example, states that in Key Stage 2 pupils should be taught to 'Explore and describe a range of beliefs, symbols and actions so that they can understand different ways of life and ways of expressing meaning'. Few people would disagree with these words but they studiously avoid stating what beliefs, symbols or actions should be taught or what meaning exactly children might be expected to understand having explored them. Describing RE in general and imprecise terms might avoid disagreements but it also leaves teachers substantially in the dark about what they should teach.

Given the diversity of schools and the lack of consensus in RE, it is probably necessary and desirable that individual schools should have a good deal of freedom when it comes to deciding on the RE content they are required to teach. This does, however, make it effectively impossible to put together an RE core curriculum which would be appropriate for all schools in a local authority or for all schools nationally.

There is, however, a compromise alternative. Just 20% of all that is taught in RE could be identified as key knowledge which all children in a local authority, or indeed nationally, should be expected to become familiar with. The remaining 80% of what schools taught in RE could be described in very broad general terms so that schools would have a good deal of latitude to interpret the requirements appropriately to meet their needs. The common 20% RE core would make it more likely that pupils moving from one phase to the next would have at least something resembling a common body of knowledge which could be built upon and deepened.

What should be in the 20% core?

What pupils should be taught in the 20% RE core is no doubt an issue on which people will have different views. However, it is not an unreasonable suggestion that all pupils should gain a secure knowledge and understanding of certain key ideas and beliefs associated with Christianity in order that they acquire an acceptable understanding of that faith.

One suggestion might be that just as all pupils are required to learn about 'Materials and Matter' in science, so all pupils through their RE lessons would be expected to learn about a central aspect of Christianity which might be called 'Easter and Salvation'. This would involve beginning in Key Stage 1 with all pupils learning about the story of the first Easter, particularly the story of Jesus' death and resurrection. As children progress, their knowledge of the first Easter should become deeper by learning about key ideas and beliefs associated with Christian phrases such as 'Jesus the Saviour', 'new life' and 'eternal life'. During Key Stage 3 pupils should build upon what they have learnt about Easter in their primary schools by learning about different atonement theories, including the 'Christus Victor' and the 'Moral Exemplar' theory, so they are able to assess these ideas for themselves and discuss them in an informed and thoughtful way.

Another area of learning that might be included in the 20% core could be the concept of 'Christian love (agape)'. In Key Stage 1 this concept might be introduced in its simplest form as it relates to sharing, giving and being kind to others. But a deeper understanding of the Christian concept of love might be developed in Key Stage 2, as pupils learn that it also includes giving up one's own time and going out of one's way to help those who may be strangers, or the marginalised, or those who are not very lovable, or, as in the story of the Good Samaritan, even one's enemies. In Key Stage 3 pupils might be helped to further deepen their understanding of the concept by learning that the giving of Christian love might involve great commitment, not expecting anything back in return, effort, personal risk, turning the other cheek, danger, even personal self-sacrifice. For many Christians, love is exemplified in its fullest sense in the God of love who enters into the world in the person of Christ and dies on the cross for the sake of all humankind.

Another area of learning that might feature in the 20% core could be to help pupils understand and appreciate Islamic ideas and beliefs associated with 'Prophethood and the Qur'an'. In Key Stage 1 pupils might learn about the story of the first revelation Muhammad received and some of the Islamic beliefs associated with the first and subsequent revelations. In Key Stage 2 pupils gain deeper knowledge and understanding by learning about important Muslim beliefs including the 'Chain of Prophets', the 'Seal of the Prophets' and how 'literal revelation' is different from 'inspirational revelation'. In Key Stage 3 pupils would explore even more deeply into Islamic beliefs, learning how the Qur'an and the Hadith and other sources or methodologies provide the basis for the Shariah. Pupils would also develop their ability to explore and discuss the authority of the Shariah and what part it plays as guidance for how a Muslim should live their daily life.

How does an RE core curriculum help assessment?

Assessment becomes a lot more straightforward if one has a well-defined content. This is because the task becomes one of finding out if what has been taught has been properly learnt. Using a system based on levels involves deciding if a pupil is demonstrating knowledge, understanding or skills against several level descriptors to see which is the 'best fit'. This in itself is quite difficult, but the task is even harder if the differences between the levels are not easy to understand. For example, what exactly is the difference between a pupil who could 'use developing religious vocabulary'(NFRE level 4) and a pupil who could 'use an increasingly wide religious vocabulary' (NFRE level 5)? Or a pupil who could 'ask important questions about religion and belief' (NFRE level 3) and a pupil who could 'raise, and suggest answers to, questions of identity, belonging, meaning, purpose, truth, values and commitments' (NFRE level 4)? Would it matter if the answers a pupil provided were plausible or were little more than ill-informed or fanciful?

Weaknesses and reservations

Assessment in RE based on core knowledge is not, however, without its weaknesses. As the RE core specified in an agreed syllabus may only include 20% of the taught content, it is not satisfactory that 80% of what is taught in RE is not also subject to a formal assessment system. There is of course no reason why a school might not follow the same principles that apply to the 20% core and specify carefully the knowledge pupils should be taught in the remaining 80% of the RE curriculum. A school will need to think carefully about what depth and progress in RE genuinely mean but the task is not impossible.

Another weakness in having an assessment system based on an RE core is the difficulty it presents when the subject matter of assessment is not strictly speaking entirely to do with knowledge or understanding about religion. Often when RE is at its best it encourages young people to consider challenging and contentious religious questions and invites pupils to express their own views and to appraise the matter for themselves. It is also made clear that pupils should not just give their views but should explain the grounds upon which their views are based. Not untypically, serious and challenging questions are asked in RE, not least because young people themselves ask such questions as they try to make sense of life and of who they are. For example, young people ask questions like:

- How do we know there is a God?
- If there is a God, why is there so much suffering and violence in the world?
- Is there a life after death?
- When this life ends, is there a better life to come?
- Must you believe in Jesus Christ to be saved?
- If there is one God, why are there so many different religions?
- Religions say different things so how can they all be true?
- Does prayer make a difference?

- Is religion a good thing?
- Does religion encourage conflict?

The quality of thinking

It could be claimed that the response young people make to questions of this kind cannot be assessed. It is just a matter of personal opinion and there are no right or wrong answers. However, it is a mistake to think that responding to challenging religious questions is similar to having personal subjective views like preferring apples to oranges or having a fondness for yellow but not blue. An examination of how people, including young people, actually answer challenging religious questions shows that there is a real difference in the quality of the answers they give. Clearly, assessment of a young person's ability when considering religious questions cannot be that they should simply be taught the 'correct' answer and that they should recall that answer and affirm it when required. Rather, assessment when it comes to contentious religious questions is not so much concerned with affirming this or that conclusion but rather with the *quality of thinking* the young person has shown which has brought them to that conclusion. Assessment in this area should, therefore, be concerned with:

- the accuracy and relevance of the information which the young person uses to support their conclusion;
- the quality of the ideas and statements made, particularly whether there is a thread which connects statements so that there is underpinning coherent logic to the argument presented;
- whether words are used consistently, whether metaphors or analogies are appropriate;
- whether evidence provided is reliable, well-sourced and corroborated. Evidence should not be merely anecdotal or hearsay, or based on scouring a text and selecting quotations out of context in order to 'prove' a point. This is a flawed rhetorical device often known as proof texting.
- understanding how humans are likely to behave or think or what motivates their actions;
- recognising that an issue may not be 'black or white' and that a young person may be aware of arguments which they are able to accurately and fairly describe and counter with arguments of their own.

When young people are expressing their views in response to challenging and contentious religious questions, assessment is a good deal more complex than ensuring that pupils can recall a religious story accurately. However, it is not impossible. Providing clear feedback and examining with pupils examples of flawed arguments, and appreciating what they look like and why they are flawed, can help children to understand what they should avoid in order to improve.

Pupils should also be given opportunities to examine well-presented arguments and have their attention drawn to what it is that makes an argument persuasive but also legitimate. Understanding what makes evidence sound and in what sense evidence may be flawed or questionable can and should be part of the taught curriculum of RE. It is possible of course that, regardless of clear feedback and good guidance, some young people may still knowingly make use of flawed arguments and dodgy evidence. Some aspects of RE, like teaching young people to have integrity and to respect evidence and reason, can be part of the taught RE curriculum and their appropriate use can be assessed. There is, of course, no guarantee they will be taken to heart and will always be applied. However, knowing and understanding the principles of presenting a sound argument in the context of a religious question are essential if pupils are to engage with important issues in a useful way.

Progression in RE

What does progression in RE look like? Since the publication of the SCAA Model Syllabuses in 1994 the terms 'learning about religion' and 'learning from religion' have been widely seen as necessary elements in any discussion of what progress in RE involves. This view was reinforced by their use in the QCA's 'Non-statutory Framework' in 2004, but in recent years their value has been questioned. However, when it comes to trying to provide a fairly clear and accurate account of what progress in RE looks like, 'learning about' and 'learning from' religion are still highly relevant.

Progress in RE isn't just the accumulation of information about religion, though this is obviously important. When the subject is done well, it is also about helping pupils to analyse, critique and evaluate religion and belief for themselves. It is about them having some skills and practical know-how so that they can weigh up matters to do with religion and belief for themselves; they can make up their own minds. They are not easy prey to what other people tell them but are, at least to some extent, on the road to becoming an autonomous thinking person.

Developing this capacity to think for oneself comes about when pupils seriously engage with religion and belief, asking challenging and difficult questions about religions, about existence itself, about what life is for and how it should be lived. They also ask difficult questions about themselves. By doing so, they emerge with a much deeper understanding of what they believe and where they stand in relation to religion and belief. In other words, they have not simply learnt about religion but have learnt from religion and are better and wiser for having done so.

Learning about religion

When it comes to learning about religion, it is possible to identify progression as involving three main steps. The first of these steps we can call 'recall'. The second step is 'description', and the third step is usually called 'understanding'.

Step 1: recall

Recall takes place when pupils show some knowledge, usually factual knowledge, about religion. For example, a young person may look at a photograph and say, 'It's a mosque', or they may recognise an artefact and say, 'It's a diva lamp'. Similarly, they may be able to recall the outline of a religious story. For example, a child may recall a simple version of the nativity story by reporting the following:

- Jesus was born in a stable. There was no room at the inn.
- Three wise men came.

This first step essentially shows disconnected knowledge. There is no evidence of an organised or connected body of knowledge but rather isolated pockets of knowledge often involving little more than single words. Rather like a dot puzzle, the dots are emerging on the page but the pupil hasn't really begun to connect up the dots.

Step 2: description

A pupil who has achieved the second step shows knowledge which is now much more coherent and sustained. The pupil has begun to develop a pattern or web of knowledge. The dots are being joined up and are no longer simply disconnected facts. However, a pupil's knowledge is still largely limited to the factual. So, for example, if shown a picture of infant baptism, or if asked about the ceremony, a pupil may connect up three or four bits of knowledge. For example:

- The man holds the baby.
- He pours water onto the baby's head.
- There is a font which has water in it.
- It takes place in a church.

The pupil may not only have an emerging picture or web of knowledge about Christianity but there may be other developing pictures of other religious traditions. As more information about religion and belief is learnt, pupils are able to attach this new information to their existing store of knowledge. So, if a pupil learns about fasting in Islam, this new information becomes linked to their existing store of knowledge about Islam, resulting in an increasingly substantial and coherent picture of that faith.

Some children with learning difficulties have real problems integrating new information about a religion. This is often because they have virtually no existing mental framework onto which they can attach any new information about a faith. An important task for the teacher of RE is to find ways of helping such pupils to mentally organise and store new information so that pupils develop a coherent picture of each religion they study and are not left simply with a jumbled and confused array of half-remembered material.

Pupils with learning difficulties often have problems with description. This can be true in oral work but is particularly evident in written activities. For example, a pupil with learning difficulties in RE may:

* omit significant information;
* use very simple sentences;
* use long and rambling sentences, e.g. repetitive use of conjunctions – 'and then';
* present information in a non-logical order;
* use certain words repetitiously, e.g. 'really nice', 'very big';
* fail to use appropriate religious vocabulary.

In order to support a child that has these sorts of difficulty the teacher of RE needs to establish whether the problem is due to limited learning about religion, in which case the child may need targeted support of a particular kind, for example:

* making information more vividly memorable;
* providing additional scaffolding to help with the ordering of information;
* providing recall activities to secure learning.

Or it may be that the child's difficulties are not primarily to do with learning about religion but have more to do with language and the organisation of ideas and information. If it is a general language difficulty, the child will be having the same sort of problems in other curriculum areas which demand similar language skills, for example English, history and geography. If it is a more general difficulty with language, perhaps particularly written language, the nature of the support the child needs is different and might include:

* encouragement to use notes or diagrams to organise information prior to writing;
* the teacher modelling the process of composition;
* sharing composition, and encouraging the pupil to join in composing;

- support for writing using writing frames or a writing partner;
- encouragement for the use of drafting and re-drafting using word processing.

Of course, often pupils with learning difficulties struggle with a complex mix of problems involving both learning about religion and difficulty with ordering and communicating information and ideas.

Step 3: understanding

The third step forward in learning about religion takes place when pupils begin to show understanding. When pupils have achieved this step, their knowledge about a religion is no longer confined to mere factual knowledge. Their knowledge is no longer limited to the overt external aspects of a religion, that is, what can be seen, heard or touched. Instead pupils now show awareness of the feelings, beliefs and emotions which are part of the experience of being religious. Pupils are no longer limited to knowledge which is about 'what', 'who', 'when' and 'where'. They are now able to offer answers which begin to explain religious life by responding effectively to 'why' questions.

For example, a person may be able to provide a sustained description of daily prayer in Islam. They may know that Muslims face in the direction of Makkah to pray, and that when they pray, they stand, bow and prostrate. The pupil may know that as Muslims make these movements, they recite particular words in Arabic. Yet, if asked why Muslims pray, a pupil may have no understanding of what prayer means to Muslims. They may not be aware of its status or significance within the faith. They may not be aware of the beliefs, emotions and feelings which Muslims associate with prayer. At the poorest level of understanding, a person may think the ritual is of little more significance than a 'keep fit' exercise involving stretching and bending or see it as just a religious duty that one undertakes with no real knowledge of what it is for or what purpose it may serve.

Children with learning difficulties often underachieve in or evade tasks which call for understanding. For example:

- They avoid a loss of self-esteem and possible failure by using responses such as 'I don't know' or by spending time on lower-order activities like description and then apparently running out of time to undertake 'understanding' activities.
- They use circular responses which beg the question, e.g. 'They do it because it's their religion'.
- They provide repetitive, non-specific responses, e.g. 'It's special to them' or 'It's holy'.

Teachers need to be aware of these strategies and respond to them effectively. It is not unusual to see children continually use limited, brief answers such as 'They feel closer to God' to a whole array of questions about religious life. It is not unknown for teachers to reward such limited answers with misplaced praise, like 'Well done,' or 'Well tried'. Or children are sometimes vaguely exhorted to strive for more insight, with comments like 'Try to say more'. It would be of more help to children if they were advised as to how they might improve their response to 'why' questions in RE. For example, children might be advised to:

- avoid the repetition of phrases such as 'it's special' or 'it's holy';
- make use of words which are more specifically used in different faith traditions, e.g. Islam – submission; Christianity – fellowship; Buddhism – compassion.

Another feature which is characteristic of this third step is that pupils' factual knowledge becomes more secure and assured. They do not have to think hard or struggle to recall factual information about different religious traditions; more often than not they recall information quickly and without hesitation. Their factual recall is also well organised so they tend not to confuse information about one religion with another.

Learning from religion

The pattern of progress in learning from religion involves primarily a growing self-awareness rather than a growth of knowledge of the world out there. This growing self-awareness takes place in two senses: 'informing their own lives' and 'forming their own judgements'.

Learning from religion – informing their own lives

A pupil may learn from religion in the sense that they increasingly see how religion may inform their own life. A child may, for example, be able to recall, describe or explain the story of 'The Good Samaritan'. By doing so, they would have demonstrated learning about religion. However, a pupil may also see ways in which the story may inform or have an application in their life. For example, they may suggest that the story is telling them that they should be kind and helpful to a person who has hurt themselves and that it would be wrong to simply walk away and ignore them. A response of this kind is often called 'personal evaluation'.

Learning from religion – forming their own judgements

A pupil may also 'learn from religion' in a second sense: the study of religion may help them to form their own judgements and arrive at a clearer and more informed understanding of their own beliefs and values. This is known as 'impersonal evaluation'.

When 'impersonal evaluation' is being undertaken, it is religion that is under the microscope and it is religion that is being evaluated. What is being assessed is not a pupil's personal beliefs. 'Learning from religion' doesn't involve telling pupils that their personal beliefs about religion are right or wrong; rather, it is the process by which they arrive at their personal beliefs which the teacher of RE is concerned with. In other words, in RE the teacher encourages pupils to express their beliefs and values and to reflect on how they arrived at their judgement. In doing so, pupils are helped to decide how they should make such judgements and so become increasingly capable of independent thinking. Assessment when it comes to 'impersonal evaluation' is not concerned with whether a pupil agrees or disagrees with what a religion may claim, but rather with the quality of the pupil's thinking which has brought them to their conclusion. For example, has the pupil taken into account any available evidence? Has the pupil made use of evidence which is well supported or is it highly selective or of questionable authority? Is the pupil's line of argument well structured and clear? Does the pupil make use of ideas and words in a way which is consistent or are there contradictions in the pupil's thinking? Has the pupil considered the views of others? Are they able to recognise weaknesses in their own argument and make a sound defence of their view in response to any weaknesses? Is the pupil aware of the consequences of their judgement? Do they show good foresight of what might happen or is their judgement based on exaggerated or unlikely claims?

When it comes to young people learning to articulate their own beliefs and values, we can again see a series of steps which shows progression.

Step 1 occurs when a pupil is uncertain of how to defend their views. They may be capable of asking significant questions like 'Is there any proof that God exists?' or 'Does prayer make a difference?', and they may be able to give their opinion in response to such questions, but as yet they do not venture answers of their own. They may be capable of expressing their opinion but they are not able to support it with a relevant or meaningful reason. For example, a pupil may use a reason that is circular, or persuasively weak, or is barely relevant, e.g. 'God exists because it's true' or 'Prayer does make a difference as some people pray every day'.

Step 2 can be seen as pupils expressing their views with simple but relevant and supportive reasons. For example, they may say things like 'God must exist because if there is no God, how did the world get made?' or 'Prayer does make a difference because I prayed for my sister to get well and she is a lot better now'.

Step 3 occurs when pupils are able to provide a more sophisticated and informed, reasoned defence of their views. A more sophisticated response may involve pupils providing multiple relevant and coherent reasons. However, what a teacher should primarily be seeking to encourage is the use of a quality reason or a limited number of quality reasons which are defended in depth, rather than a quantity of reasons of which none are very strong or well supported. This kind of more sophisticated thinking is seen when pupils are able to support their reasons using a series of connective statements which have an underpinning logic. Pupils typically avoid anecdotal evidence but use:

- stronger and more authoritative evidence;
- appropriate narratives, examples or analogies to clarify their argument;
- contrary arguments, offering a sound defence against such objections;
- authorities or principles which are likely to have widespread appeal.

Before young people even begin to make any of these steps, there are earlier indications of progress in RE. For example, a pupil may demonstrate progress by listening attentively to the telling of a religious story, or they may show some self-awareness by reflecting on what makes them happy or sad. These earlier steps are well described in the P levels in religious education.

In order to begin to establish an effective assessment strategy which will help children with learning difficulties, it is necessary to involve pupils and actively give them some responsibility. Just as the classroom teacher needs to know what 'making progress' in RE means, so do the pupils. Sharing with pupils the local agreed syllabus levels or statements may help, but usually the language is so daunting that pupils cannot respond to them. Breaking down and simplifying the local standards into language the pupils can understand can help a great deal. But likely to be of even more help is providing and discussing with them examples of what pupils have said or written when they have demonstrated depth of knowledge and understanding of aspects to do with religion or belief, or, similarly, examples of what pupils have said or written when they have shown a capacity to produce a sustained, well-reasoned and balanced argument in response to questions about religion or belief.

5 Managing support

A valuable resource

Over the last ten years or so, as schools have gained more responsibility for managing their own budgets, there has been a substantial increase in the number of adult support staff at work in classrooms. Many of these are trained teaching assistants (TAs). The teacher of RE, just like the teacher of any other curriculum area, is wasting a valuable resource if they do not make effective use of the adult support made available to them. It is still the case that, aside from a nod or a brief 'hello', a teaching assistant may be largely ignored by the mainstream classroom teacher. Sadly, this can be just as true in the RE classroom as any curriculum area.

Wider contribution

Often a teaching assistant may have a central brief to support a particular child or group of children who have special needs. However, in addition to that, many TAs understand their role in a much wider sense and are able and very willing to contribute to the quality of teaching and learning generally in the classroom. This can come about through the initiative of the teaching assistant. It is not unknown for a teaching assistant to enter into a contemporary RE classroom with little more than their childhood memory of RE, or a memory of Sunday School classes, informing their expectations. Nevertheless, they quickly discover an unexpected world of religious diversity and thoughtful discussion. They may find the non-confessional aims of modern RE very appealing, so much so that they feel that they can and do wish to contribute to lessons more actively.

Although adult support staff may recognise the aims of the teacher of RE by observing what is happening in the classroom, it is usually better not to leave this unsaid, expecting the TA to surmise what is going on. Well before the lesson starts, it is of great help if the teacher of RE can spend some time providing a brief outline of what the lesson is about and what they are trying to achieve. This enables the adult support staff to understand the lesson and puts them in a much better position to make a valuable contribution.

For example, in a lesson about murtis or images of gods used in Hinduism the support staff might think that the main aim of the lesson is to develop accurate observation and recall. Believing this to be the case, the teaching assistant might ask the pupils they are working with to note how many arms or heads the image in front of them may have and be satisfied if they answer correctly. The teacher, however, may be much more interested in encouraging the pupils to explore religious symbolism and in inviting pupils to consider what the image may be saying about the power of the divine symbolised by the image's many arms. Or the teacher may be interested in the belief that God has an all-seeing awareness of everything, symbolised by the many heads and eyes shown in the image. Of course, many observant teaching assistants can work out for themselves what the teacher is trying to achieve in the course of the lesson and improvise appropriate ways of supporting them. But a proper and professional discussion between the teacher and the teaching assistant prior to the lesson can help remove any misunderstanding and maximise learning opportunities.

Many teaching assistants will be able to draw upon their training and find ways of supporting the teacher of RE during the course of the lesson. However, it is well worthwhile providing examples of how situations can be developed as they arise.

Encouraging reticent pupils

The teacher may show the class a number of images of mosques around the world and invite the pupils to comment on the dome as a common feature. Susan, a very shy girl who rarely speaks, may mutter, 'They look like onions.' The TA encourages Susan to speak up: 'Go on, Susan, tell the class.' Susan repeats what she has said for the rest of the class to hear. This proves to be a very helpful contribution to the lesson. The teacher points out that the curves and shapes of natural objects like onions and leaves are often used in Islam. Symmetry and the replication of pattern are often a feature of nature and it is no accident that they are typically a feature of Islamic art and architecture. The children go on to learn that in Islam the examples of symmetry and the curves of nature are quite often used when building mosques as this is believed to add to the beauty of the building. Muslims believe that by drawing upon nature for inspiration they are paying a compliment to God as they are using the same beautiful examples of design to be seen in nature that God himself designed and used when creating the universe.

With pupils who lack confidence in speaking out and answering questions, the TA can help them in a number of different ways:

- rehearsing their response (to give them confidence) before they speak out;
- alerting the teacher so that the teacher knows the pupil has an answer and can ask the pupil by name;
- helping the pupil to write down a short answer on an individual white board to hold up;
- speaking for the pupil (but wherever possible encouraging the pupil to speak for themselves).

Dropping helpful pointers

The class are invited to look at an image showing the earth from space. Working in pairs, pupils are asked to think of a question the image raises for them. Shelley suggests that the planet looks 'lonely'. Her partner Dylan agrees, saying that the planet looks 'all on its own in the dark'. After a long pause the TA asks, 'If we are alone in the dark, could we go and live anywhere else?' The pupils talk about pollution, the ozone layer and living on another planet. After a while the two pupils come up with the question, 'What must we do to save our planet from becoming too polluted for humans to live on?'

Developing pupils' thinking skills is an important part of the TA role but one that is not always understood. Too often, the TA will 'put words into their mouths'; instead, useful prompts can be used to encourage pupils to think more and/ or more broadly:

Figure 5.1 A teaching assistant can provide helpful pointers.

© Fox Lane Photography

- What else can you see/say about this?
- Why do you say/think that?
- Can you think of another example of . . .?

Reminding pupils of connections between new and previous learning is also valuable.

Starting the ball rolling

During a lesson on Jesus' concern for the outcast and the marginalised, based on the story of Jesus and Matthew the tax-collector, pupils in groups of three are asked to draw up a list of people who may feel outcast or rejected today. After a long pause the group seem unable to come up with any ideas. The TA invites the pupils to think about recent news reports about people who are suffering or are in difficulty. The group start their list with 'refugees' and then add 'young people with no jobs', then 'the homeless' and 'the elderly'.

Playing 'devil's advocate'

In groups of four the pupils are asked to discuss, 'What are the top things in life that bring happiness?' The group appear to largely agree, suggesting things like 'friends', 'being loved' and 'having a family'. The TA joins in, saying, 'Get real . . . you need pots of money. Money can buy you happiness.' The discussion becomes more enlivened as the group counters the TA's contribution. Aaliyah, who normally says very little, is asked by the TA what she thinks and she replies, 'Well, every day you hear about people who are filthy rich but they have booze problems, drug problems, they are overweight, underweight, they fight with their partners. Money doesn't seem to have made them very happy.'

Echoing the teacher

In a series of lessons called 'Religion and the Rights of Women', pupils are asked to write a short statement giving their personal view on the question 'Are Muslims right to ban beauty queen contests?' Sukvey writes a descriptive account of what traditional Muslim clothing for women looks like. The TA reminds Sukvey, 'Remember to give your personal view. Are Muslims right or wrong to ban beauty queen contests?'

Pupils with SEND can 'miss the point' sometimes and go off at a tangent; reminding them of the learning objective and focus of the task provides valuable support.

Demonstrating for the teacher

The teacher explores with the pupils gestures used in Islam to symbolise respect for the Qur'an, such as washing hands before touching a Qur'an, wrapping the book in a cloth, placing it on a high shelf for safe keeping, placing it carefully on a wooden stand off the floor for reading. As the teacher explains each of these gestures, the TA provides a demonstration.

This type of team teaching can also raise the status of a TA in the eyes of pupils, resulting in a greater respect for them and thereby increasing their efficacy.

TAs can also help with the management of behaviour in an RE classroom, as in the following examples.

Sitting alongside a difficult child

Unnoticed by the teacher, Shane may make several quiet verbal asides which distract or give offence to other children. For example, 'Look at him! He's got a tea towel around his head!' The TA changes position and sits closer to Shane. Shane recognises the signal and moderates his behaviour.

It is a great advantage to a teacher when there is 'another pair of eyes' in the classroom. If the TA is alert and can spot this sort of misdemeanor and 'nip it in the bud', they can prevent escalation and possible disruption of the lesson.

Troubleshooting

Georgina is becoming frustrated as the Passover bread (matzah) and mixture of apples, nuts, wine and cinnamon (haroset), placed on her table for the group to taste, has been eaten by other people in her group. The TA collects some more Passover bread and haroset from the teacher's desk and brings it to the table for Georgina to taste.

Supporting children who need specific help to access the lesson

Ricky has a particular difficulty with writing and often puts off getting started by using various avoidance activities, like distracting other pupils and leaving his seat to ask other pupils for a pen. The TA sits next to Ricky and encourages him to speak out loud his first sentence rather than write it down. The subject is Sikhism and arranged marriage. Ricky says, 'Well . . . arranged marriages seem strange but they work. Don't they!' With some further encouragement Ricky writes the first sentence: 'Arranged marriages may seem strange but many Sikhs find that they work.' With the aid of a spell-checker the TA helps Ricky to spell 'arranged', 'strange' and 'Sikhs'. The TA encourages Ricky to think about what else he can say by asking, 'If parents are involved in suggesting who their son or daughter might marry, why might that be a good idea?' Ricky replies, 'They might know you better than you know yourself.' The TA suggests that idea could be used to write the next sentence.

Acting as a 'thinking partner'

During a lesson about Judaism and the Commandments the pupils are asked to think of a law that they would like to see passed. They are given two minutes' quiet thinking time. Adam draws a doodle. The TA asks Adam, 'What law would you like to see passed, Adam?' Adam replies, 'Dunno.' 'Is there one thing in your street, in the playground, in the park, by the shops, anywhere, which could be made better?' 'Yeah,' says Adam, 'it should be a law to say you can go quad bike racing.' After further discussion Adam comes up with a law which grants funding to faith groups and non-governmental organisations to provide facilities and coaching in extreme sports for young people.

Management of resources

TAs can also help with the management of resources in the RE classroom. They can help a lesson move with pace and avoid loss of concentration by distributing pencils or paper, holding up prompt cards, reading an extract from a book or perhaps operating equipment, as in the following example.

In a lesson which examines how God is discussed in contemporary music, the pupils are to hear extracts from four separate songs. The first is Van Morrison and Cliff Richard singing 'Whenever God Shines His Light', which describes God as a strength in a crisis. This is to be followed by Madonna's 'Like a Prayer', which describes God as a mystery over which she has no control. The third song is Pink's use of the metaphor 'God is a DJ', followed by George Harrison's sense of joy and love expressed in 'My Sweet Lord'. In between each song there is to be time for pupils to analyse and discuss. Each song extract is played back on the computer and the lyrics are shown on the whiteboard. In order to try to bring about a seamless flow to the discussion, the teacher asks the TA to operate the computer and cue up each song when signalled.

Assessment and feedback

Teaching assistants can provide valuable information about what a particular child, or group of children, may have learnt during a lesson. We know that there is often a substantial gap between what teachers teach and what pupils learn.

A TA working closely with individual children may be able to identify how or why a child has failed to understand. Or they may observe that a child has distorted a particular idea, in a way of which the teacher may be quite unaware. For example, a teacher may have provided an excellent account of how Muhammad is believed by Muslims to be a prophet and that this is not the same as the Christian belief that Jesus is the Christ. A TA, while supporting children with special learning difficulties, may recognise that several of these children have not understood the distinction between 'The Prophet' and 'Christ' correctly. When questioned, the children say things like 'Muhammad is very special to Muslims, like Jesus is very special to Christians'.

Feedback from the TA about whether an idea has been understood, or lost in transmission, should be treated by the teacher as gold dust. If children are to learn effectively, the teacher of RE must know what has been understood, what has to be revisited and how an idea may have to be tackled differently so as to avoid confusion. In order to encourage such feedback it is advisable for teachers to:

- provide briefing prior to a lesson – anticipating how an idea or a concept may be incorrectly grasped by children, brief the TA appropriately, prior to the lesson, so that they are alerted as to how children may fail to learn correctly;
- actively encourage feedback from the TA – TAs can often be reluctant to give feedback to teachers even if they are very aware that children in the class have been completely unable to undertake a task or have failed to grasp vital information. They may fear that such observations will be regarded by the teacher as unwelcome criticisms. Teachers do need to make it clear that they value the TA's observations and that any post-analysis of a lesson will not be resented or treated in a cursory way. 'Sticky notes' are commonly used by TAs to make short comments about pupils that they attach to the teacher's mark book at the end of a lesson, or to the pupil's book when handed in for marking. This facilitates good communication even when the TA has to hurry away to the next lesson.

First-hand knowledge of a religious tradition

A TA may well have almost unique, first-hand knowledge about a particular faith community. Such first-hand knowledge can be a tremendous asset in the RE classroom. With a little encouragement a TA may be persuaded to give a ten-minute presentation, either to a group of children or perhaps to the whole class, on topics like:

- our family's celebration of Baisakhi;
- my church group's annual visit to Lourdes;

- my daughter's confirmation and first communion;
- what it is like to fast during Ramadan;
- how we pray at a Quaker meeting;
- Puja and our family shrine to Krishna;
- my ten day visit to Israel/Palestine.

First-hand religious experience

Many people, and TAs are no exception, may have a fascinating story to tell about a spiritual or religious experience. Their story may have little to do with an explicit religious tradition. Nevertheless, if they are prepared to share the details of their experience in the classroom, it can help bring alive for young people a real awareness of what often drives faith and commitment. Young people obviously have to be prepared for such stories and made aware that respecting the deeply held views and experiences of others is important. Having said that, young people are often very receptive to first-hand accounts of events such as those listed below:

- **a conversion experience** – perhaps following a period of some anxiety, an individual discovers reassurance and peace and senses the reality of God in their life;
- **a religious experience** – perhaps while having a country walk, an individual may have a mystical or a religious experience. For example, a person

  - hears an inner voice;
  - senses a presence;
  - has an out-of-body experience;
  - receives a message from a deceased friend;
  - senses a benevolent presence;
  - has a deep feeling that nature is a unity;
  - senses that in life everything will be okay;

- **a spiritual journey** – an individual may have a story to tell of how their faith over the years has changed. Perhaps in childhood they accepted the teaching of their Catholic upbringing. Later in life they rebelled and found some satisfaction in a branch of Hinduism and eastern meditation. However, today they are generally sceptical and would describe themselves as an atheist.

Social or community action

Some adult support staff may have experience in full- or part-time work for a charity or a community action project. Many such organisations are supported by people with a strong social conscience and have their roots in religious faith. A personal account of the day-to-day work, together with an attempt to explain something of the motives for getting involved, can provide the basis for a fascinating RE lesson. For example, adult support staff can provide a valuable slot in an RE lesson based on their

- part-time work as a Samaritan;
- Saturday morning work in a Sue Ryder shop;
- VSO work in Uttar Pradesh;
- sponsored cycle ride for Mencap;
- previous employment in a hospice;
- knowledge of a relative who has had to face the challenge of disability;
- friends' experience of drug abuse.

Holidays and visits

Adult support staff, like many people today, are often reasonably well travelled. Clearly an RE lesson should be more than an indulgent look at an adult's holiday snaps. Nevertheless, with some thought and planning, and in the right setting, visits enjoyed by TAs both in the UK and abroad can make a valuable contribution to an RE lesson, for example:

- celebrating Eid in Cairo;
- visiting the Great Mosque in Tunis;
- the day I went to Benares;
- Mardi Gras in Rio de Janeiro;
- the Passion Play in Oberammergau.

At the heart of these points is the principle of drawing TAs into the lesson in order to improve the learning process. Clearly this requires discussion and planning before the lesson begins. A rushed chat over coffee, three minutes before the lesson is due to start, is hardly likely to lead to the sharing of ideas and the professional discussion that is desired. When it comes to supporting children with learning difficulties, working with individual targets in mind can help. However, with the teacher and the TA working in partnership and identifying learning activities and specific targets for each lesson, a much better learning opportunity can be created and more genuine progress achieved.

6 Real pupils in real classrooms

We have so far looked generally at some of the issues which arise, and also at some of the strategies which might be used, in helping children that have special educational needs to make progress in RE. However, successful teaching is nearly always about understanding the needs of particular children and knowing what to do individually to develop their learning.

In this chapter we will look at case studies of individual children. Each case focuses on a particular type of educational need (it may be a child with a visual impairment, or it may be a child that has an emotional and a behaviour disorder) and offers some advice on how best to teach that child. Each case study has three sections: 'You will need to find out . . .', 'You should consider . . .' and 'Some strategies you or the TA could try'.

Effective teaching depends substantially upon the establishment of a relationship and a rapport between teacher and pupil. Being aware of a young person's educational need or of their particular impairment is important if you hope to teach them effectively. However, of even more importance is the individual pupil – their likes and dislikes, their interests and hopes, their wishes and their fears. Every teacher will do well not to lose sight of the fact that through little conversations with children, by showing interest, by avoiding sarcasm or ridicule, by the giving of time, vital ingredients like trust and respect can be established. Without that trust and respect, trying to help another person learn will always be an uphill struggle.

Kuli Y7 – hearing impairment

You will need to find out . . .

The degree of hearing loss Kuli has; for example, Kuli may have been diagnosed as having mild hearing loss. It may be, however, that Kuli's hearing impairment is much greater, in which case he may have been diagnosed as having moderate, severe or even profound hearing impairment.

You need also to find out if Kuli has his own personal FM radio-mike system. It may be that Kuli has such equipment but is uncomfortable using it and is reluctant to ask teachers to wear the mike. It may be that Kuli finds his FM system helpful but also has to rely substantially on his ability to decipher various visual clues such as facial expressions and body language, and also on some lip-reading skill. Even with all that data it may be the case that Kuli misses crucial detail and is occasionally uncertain regarding instructions. It may also be the case that Kuli is reluctant to admit that he does not always follow what is going on and has a tendency to cover up, feign understanding and only rarely ask for help.

Kuli's greatest difficulty may be in following the contributions made by others in the classroom who, when speaking, are not wearing the radio-mike. It may be that Kuli is experiencing RE which puts less emphasis on knowledge or ideas which come from the teacher. Instead, the expectation is that the pupils should contribute and show a willingness to clarify their own thoughts, ideas and views and share these with the other pupils. Kuli may therefore be finding that, particularly during open discussion, there can be lively interchanges, and comments may come from unexpected members of the class. On such occasions Kuli may be experiencing difficulty in following all of the contributions and so rarely feels able to join in himself.

IEP targets

You also need to find out if Kuli has any kind of individual support plan. Individual education plans (IEPs) are not mentioned in the latest SEND Code of Practice (January 2015). However, in the Code there are three particularly important principles and they are:

- High expectations – teachers should set high expectations to meet the needs of children and young people with SEND.
- Set ambitious targets – teachers should use appropriate assessment to set targets and these should be deliberately ambitious targets.
- Child and parent participation – the child and the child's parents should participate as fully as possible in decisions, and they should be provided with the information and support necessary to enable them to participate in those decisions.

In response to these three principles many schools find that IEPs are effective and so continue to use them. Other schools make use of ways of providing robust target setting, monitoring and recording processes for all pupils which do not involve the use of an IEP. Schools that are under local authority control are advised to find out what documentation their LA expects to receive if a school or a parent seeks a statutory assessment which may lead to the writing of an education, health and care (EHC) plan. This may help schools to decide whether to use IEPs or adopt a different type of 'graduated approach'.

If Kuli does have an individual plan, targets should be clearly stated, for example:

1. Work with a learning partner to ensure that instructions are understood.
2. Vary the learning partner in order to widen social opportunities.
3. Make at least one oral contribution in each lesson.

You should consider . . .

Regular consultation

In order to try to provide the best possible learning environment for Kuli you may wish to set up regular consultation meetings. This normally would involve the RE teacher setting aside some time every two or three weeks or so in order to consult with Kuli about his learning. Often this results in the student gaining confidence and gives them a sense that they have a voice in how they can make progress. It can also provide useful feedback for the teacher and may help them to reduce or even eliminate unconscious habits, for example:

- continuing to speak while turning to write on the board;
- standing in front of a window, creating a silhouette which hinders visual clues;
- leaving an OHP or perhaps an inkjet printer switched on when not in use, resulting in unnecessary background noise.

The room layout

Various classroom layouts and seating positions might be considered and a number of trials undertaken to see what works best. For example, it may be that by moving his seating position Kuli is able to avoid the movement of other members of the class or to move closer to the teacher and so hear more clearly. Or it may be the case that with a little experimentation a horseshoe formation proves to be the most helpful layout enabling Kuli to observe most visual clues. Or it may be that during discussion the horseshoe formation can be quickly turned into a circle and that this greatly helps Kuli's ability to see who is speaking and to understand what is being said.

Some strategies you or the TA could try

Written information

Kuli may be provided with crucial written information either at the beginning of or at certain appropriate moments in the course of the lesson. For example, Kuli may find it helpful to have

- an outline of the lesson, including the main aims;
- a list of any new words which will be introduced in the course of the lesson;
- any special class instructions, for example a key question to be considered, e.g. 'In the story of Rama and Sita what lessons might be learnt from Rama?';
- a homework assignment.

A learning partner

A shortlist of learning partners for Kuli might be drawn up. The use of learning partners may help Kuli eliminate occasional uncertainties about instructions. Learning partners may also help Kuli keep track of class discussions so that Kuli is better able to understand who is speaking and what is being said. As Kuli gains more confidence using a learning partner, a more random way of selecting members of the class to work with Kuli may be tried, in order to extend Kuli's social skills.

A word picture

Increasingly, sound may be used in an RE classroom in order to support learning. For example, students may experience

- a passage from the Qur'an being read;
- the sound of a gospel choir;
- the chanting of a Chazan reading the Torah;
- reflection supported by oriental sitar music.

When sound is being used in a major way to support learning, you may find that, rather than simply ignoring Kuli on such occasions, it is possible to provide Kuli with a written word-picture of the sound. For example:

A female soloist sings out the words:

Oh happy day, oh happy day
When Jesus washed, when Jesus washed
My sins away
He taught me how, he taught me how
To love and pray.

A full choir joins in echoing each line the soloist sings.

There is a sense of gusto, power, life and great joy in the singing.

There is a powerful drumbeat and a lively melody giving the piece a modern rock sound.

Such a strategy may of course be a limited substitute, but Kuli may well report that this is better than simply being ignored or pretending that there isn't a problem.

Harry Y7 – specific learning difficulties

You will need to find out . . .

Harry may have a lot of ability in RE. However, this may not be at all evident to his RE teacher. Particularly in the first few weeks and months of pupils arriving in a secondary school, RE teachers often find themselves with very little in the way of useful information to make an adequate assessment of a pupil's ability in RE. Evidence such as oral contributions, engagement in classroom activities and information specific to RE from the primary feeder school might all be in short supply.

Because of this, teachers of RE often make an initial assessment of a pupil's ability based on what data is available to them. In the first weeks of life in a secondary school this is often limited to a pupil's written work, for example homework or assignments undertaken during lessons. The evidence available to the teacher of RE may be writing assignments which are unfinished, low productivity, writing which is confused or poorly organised and words which are erratically or perhaps bizarrely spelt.

Viewing this evidence, teachers of RE have to identify those pupils who

- are poorly motivated – these are pupils who underachieve in RE but in other curriculum areas respond much more positively and produce work of a much higher standard;
- have a general learning difficulty – these are pupils who have a general cognitive difficulty and so find it hard to recall or organise information, or understand ideas or grasp concepts. Because of this general difficulty they are almost certainly also having difficulty with other subjects which require cognitive skills.
- have a specific learning difficulty – this is the situation with Harry. Harry in his RE lessons is not being 'sloppy' or 'uncooperative'. Nor is he necessarily of limited ability in RE. He could be highly gifted. The problem is that

Harry is being asked to undertake assignments in RE primarily through the medium of the written word, and Harry's problem is specifically with the written word, not with RE.

Diagnostic analysis

Harry's specific learning difficulty with words needs to be diagnostically analysed. This means that the school needs to find out what strategies Harry uses when he is asked to write – for example, how he plans, how he sets about composition, how he attempts to spell, what sort of errors he makes and what might be the source of those errors. The school should also look at how Harry revises his work, whether in fact he ever redrafts his work, and if so what he does during the redrafting stage.

You should consider . . .

Scaffolding writing

It may be that Harry's greatest difficulty when faced with a writing assignment is that he has a problem getting started. In order to help him develop his skill and build his confidence, it may be necessary to provide writing tasks which are very clear and structured. This may take the form of providing scaffolding or a skeleton. For example:

When I entered the Sikh gurdwara I thought . . . .

. . . .

Inside I saw . . . .

. . . .

The thing that struck me most . . . .

. . . .

One thing our Sikh guide said . . . .

. . . .

Later on we visited the langar, where . . . .

. . . .

Sikhs believe . . . .

. . . .

What I gained most from the visit was . . . .

. . . .

Fluency and repetition

It may be that Harry has a tendency to write in short sentences so that his work lacks fluency. For example:

They pray every day.
They face Makkah.
They pray to Allah.
It is a commandment.
It is in the Qur'an.

Harry may need particular help so that he learns how sentences can be combined. He may need assistance in order for him to recognise how his writing is repetitious and how this can be overcome. For example:

Muslims pray to Allah every day. When they pray they always face Makkah. The commandment to pray is found in the Qur'an.

Writing as a process

It may be the case that Harry needs to be encouraged to think that, when undertaking a writing task, he is not expected to produce an accurate and neat product at the first attempt. Writing should be seen as a process that begins with talking over ideas and sketching out some initial thoughts. Work can be edited and revised several times. In support of this idea of writing as a process, Harry's RE teacher may wish to encourage him not to use an exercise book but to use a loose-leaf folder. This will make it possible for Harry not to be always reminded of past failures but to store final drafts in which he can take pride. (See Appendix 7 for notes about the writing process.)

If a word processor can be accessed, this can be of enormous help to Harry. It will enable him to edit, erase and refine his work through several drafts, achieving a final quality product.

Some strategies you or the TA could try . . .

Specific strategies for overcoming difficulties with spelling

Harry may have a real difficulty with spelling. He may spell some words quite erratically but nevertheless show some awareness of a correspondence between letter patterns and sound, for example 'becos' (because), 'bibel' (Bible), 'juwes' (Jews). However, some words may be spelt in a much more bizarre way as he mistakes the letter name for the sound, for example 'gsos' (Jesus) or 'yl' (while). These sorts of difficulties are unlikely to correct themselves unless the issue is faced and Harry is explicitly taught spelling skills. Indeed, unless tackled the problem is likely to get worse as Harry may increasingly find his spelling embarrassing and simply withdraw as a 'reluctant writer' or become angry and frustrated and develop a behaviour problem.

Strategies that may help Harry improve his spelling:

- Draw up a list of words Harry frequently misspells. Some of these may be general words 'sed' (said), but some may be more specific to RE, e.g. 'religous' (religious), 'Buddism' (Buddhism), 'gud' (good), 'beleve' (believe).
- Establish a systematic programme of learning a list of words Harry frequently misspells.
- Encourage Harry to make an active effort to remember every detail of a targeted word. Harry should look carefully at how the word should be spelt, but also he should look carefully at how he tends to misspell the word.
- While speaking the word, quietly practise writing the word from memory. Attempt to learn each word by eye, ear and hand, not just by eye alone. See the word, say the word, feel the word, write the word. (See the 'look, say, cover, write, check' prompt in Appendix 6.)
- Make use of a progress chart in order to plot the number of new words learnt each week.
- Make use of an electronic spell-checker so as to avoid frustration when writing.

Megan Y10 – wheelchair user

You will need to find out . . .

Consultation

Consultation should be a major feature of a school's educational provision for Megan, and this applies just as much in the RE classroom as elsewhere. The fact that Megan has a mobility impairment does not mean that she has a similar impairment when it comes to speaking, learning, thinking or feeling. It is important not to patronise, condescend or make assumptions about Megan's preferences without exploring her views on the matter.

Physical access

If Megan's RE lessons are taking place in a classroom she hasn't used before, it will be necessary to find out if this is presenting her with unforeseen access problems. Obvious modifications like ramps, lifts and toilet facilities may be in place generally within the school. However, Megan may be encountering particular access problems which she should be consulted about in order that improvements or solutions can be found.

Megan should also be consulted about where she wishes to place herself in the classroom. She may, for example, find it helpful if an easily accessible space in the classroom is reserved.

Preferences as a learner

It will also be necessary to find out Megan's particular strengths and weaknesses as a learner. It is important when looking at Megan not only to see the wheelchair but also to see Megan as a young person with her own particular strengths and weaknesses and preferences as a learner. She may principally use mind-mapping, pictures and diagrams to grasp and communicate ideas. It may be that she has a strong social conscience and a particular interest in moral issues, or in evangelical Christianity, or in questions about existence and destiny, in which case this information may be just as important, perhaps more important, to bear in mind when teaching Megan than anything to do with her as a wheelchair user.

You should consider . . .

When teaching Megan there are a number of dos and don'ts which you should consider. These may not be very specific to religious education but they are nevertheless important. For example:

- When talking to Megan, sit beside her so that your eyes are at the same level.
- Sit free of Megan's wheelchair and avoid leaning on it. Megan may well regard her wheelchair as part of her personal space.
- Don't assume that Megan needs assistance, for example in accessing resources or equipment. She may well enjoy exercising her independence and not want others always doing things for her.
- At the same time, be alert in case Megan does need assistance – for example, with accessing books or resources which are on a high shelf, carrying objects or holding a door open.

- Give consideration to how Megan can best be helped to participate in classroom strategies which anticipate movement around the classroom – for example, forming a discussion circle, undertaking a role-play, forming a group to work with.
- Also give consideration to how Megan can participate in visits and out-of-school activities, such as visiting a local synagogue or undertaking a survey on local attitudes to religion.
- If Megan is being prepared for some form of national accreditation in RE, find out if the examining authority permits additional time or rest breaks. This is likely to depend on Megan's specific disability. Advice can usually be gained from the examination board's examination officer, and it is possible that medical evidence may be required.

Some strategies you or the TA could try

As pupils enter into Key Stage 4, it is increasingly likely that they will be undertaking an RE course which is intended to prepare them for some form of national accreditation. Although success in a religious studies GCSE or religious studies Entry Level might seem like incentive enough from the point of view of the teacher, this is not necessarily the view adopted by students. The exam carrot is not enough. Instead, the most successful Key Stage 4 RE teaching programmes attempt to engage pupils by following a few guidelines such as those outlined below.

Minimise writing

Writing which is little more than note-taking (on the grounds that this is needed for revision purposes) is often resented by young people, including young people who are wheelchair users. If essential information has to be made available, it is better to provide printed copies of such information which students may read and store for future reference.

Encourage discussion

RE provides many opportunities for young people to engage in discussion in order that they can learn how to form and articulate their views. Teachers of RE should maximise opportunities for such discussion. Megan may need some encouragement in discussions, but all participants should be made aware of certain rules like

- listening to others;
- taking turns;
- using the language of courtesy.

Class discussions nearly always go better if

- the subject under discussion is topical and relevant;
- the students have had some say about the question or motion to be discussed;
- the contributions from very vocal individuals are restricted, encouraging less confident students to make a contribution;
- the teacher makes it clear that they are an 'active listener' to the discussion and not an 'active participant' wishing to push the discussion towards a particular conclusion.

Vary the format

Attempt to plan lessons which take the students by surprise by avoiding the same format or routines. Role-play may seem like a novel way to learn, but if role-play becomes a repeated strategy it quickly becomes predictable and loses its impact. Attempt to surprise your students with

- **visiting speakers** – a local hospital chaplain explains their day-to-day work;
- **problem-solving** – should Mr and Mrs Williams have their baby baptised?
- **mock trials** – the British media on trial: 'Is it guilty of demonising Islam?';
- **an imaginary TV interview** – 'If Jesus were alive today', the David Dimbleby Interview;
- **expert in role** – an atheist scientist on the origin of life;
- **design an advert** – plan a twenty-five second TV advert for Buddhism.

In all these activities Megan should be encouraged to play a full and active part. She should be given opportunities to take a lead – and not be seen merely as someone who is helped out by making sure she has a good view of what others in the classroom are doing.

Steven Y8 – social, emotional and mental health difficulties

You will need to find out . . .

Steven may show his emotional and behavioural disorder in a variety of ways. The teacher of RE may find that Steven has a range of difficulties which lead to aggressive and disruptive behaviour. For example, he may

- be very impulsive;
- easily become distracted, restless and inattentive;
- have poor social relationships;
- often be off-task, use verbal abuse or verbally bait other students or the teacher;
- be threatening, physically aggressive, easily angered, violent.

All too often pupils who exhibit such behaviour have traumatic lives outside school in which tension and aggression are the norm. In such an environment a young person may become destructive and rebellious. They may have difficulty in establishing close relationships and suffer from low self-esteem. Knowledge of Steven's home circumstances can be a revelation to some of his teachers and may help them to arrive at a much more balanced assessment of his behaviour.

However, even if Steven does have a very difficult home background, that does not mean that the situation is hopeless and nothing can be done. Research into effective schools indicates that schools can play a major role in either helping or hindering young people with emotional and behavioural difficulties.

RE teachers that are most effective in teaching young people like Steven usually find that their task is made easier when they teach in schools which have

- an effective senior management which provides direction for all staff – they take an interest in RE and support the subject, particularly in terms of time-tabling, accommodation and staffing, and are committed to the development of good-quality teaching and learning;
- a whole-school policy on behaviour;
- a 'critical mass' of staff that support and practise the school's behaviour policy.

You will need to know if there is a policy in the school if Steven, or pupils like Steven, harass or bully other children. For example, is there a 'cool-off zone' or a 'time-out plan' and, if there is, how does it operate? Does Steven have an 'individual behaviour plan' or a 'contract' and, if not, does the school have a system in place for generating one? Has the school in place a system for teaching Steven anger-management skills? Has Steven been advised about what he should do if he finds himself getting angry or how he might avoid such a situation arising? Are there prescribed classroom rules covering situations in which Steven typically may be experiencing difficulty? For example, are there clear rules like 'lining up', 'coming in' or 'going out' rules? Does the school have 'talking', 'hands up', 'swearing', 'eating', 'arriving late' or 'coats off' rules? Are these rules being applied consistently throughout the school? Does Steven need additional support or training in order that he understands these rules and what is expected of him?

Or is the expectation perhaps that each teacher will negotiate such rules for themselves with each of their classes, in order to encourage ownership of the rules? As RE often involves discussion of controversial or sensitive issues, it can be useful for every teacher of RE to negotiate with their classes a suitable 'positive language rule' or a 'non-put-down rule' or a 'racist language rule'.

You should consider . . .

A behaviour profile

It may be that a real step forward in helping Steven to manage his behaviour can be achieved if a 'behaviour profile' of Steven is undertaken. A 'behaviour profile' is a formal study of Steven's behaviour. For example, is Steven disruptive in virtually all of his lessons, or is it just RE and one or two other lessons? Does Steven have particular bad-days? For example, is there a pattern of misbehaviour on Mondays or Fridays, or on afternoons, or following particular lessons?

Curriculum design

Even if Steven's disruptive behaviour is not confined just to RE, it is still necessary to make sure that the RE curriculum design is appropriate. Some RE schemes of work continue to contain areas of study which are of doubtful relevance to many young people today. It may be that Steven is particularly rebellious if he is expected to learn about the geography of ancient Israel, or become familiar with ancient Polynesian creation stories, or explain what difference there may be between an Ansate, a Maltese, a Celtic, a Papal and a Lorraine cross.

Far from reinforcing knowledge, some RE tasks, like 'Draw a picture of Jesus' entry into Jerusalem', 'Copy out the words of the Muslim call to prayer' or 'Decorate your Succoth Card with Jewish symbols', are little more than ways of keeping young people occupied while the clock ticks down. Frustration at his inability to draw Jesus on a donkey, and his feeling that, even if he could, what purpose would it serve, could be a contributory factor in Steven's distracted behaviour and frequent task refusal.

Some strategies you or the TA could try

Steven's behaviour may be aggravated by poor classroom management. RE teachers are not saints and, just like any other human being, an RE teacher may find themselves aggravated by Steven's behaviour. Arising from a trivial incident, Steven may swear and react aggressively, 'Give me back my pen you s _ _.' He may engage in argument and back-chat of defiance, 'I'm not talking! You're always picking on me. I'm not working with her!' The temptation is to think that you must use counter-power to show that you are in charge. The teacher may feel that what is needed in such a situation is an angry and loud retort, 'How dare you talk like that in my classroom!' Many teachers think that by a demonstration of their power Steven will get the message and this will correct his behaviour.

By showing reactive anger are you helping to defuse the situation? Or are you, by entering into a power struggle with Steven, backing him in public into a corner, which simply increases the tension and only makes the situation worse? There are alternative strategies and ways of managing anger and avoiding possible conflict. For example, avoid shouting or yelling at or threatening Steven. This usually will only result in more hostility and anger from Steven and is very likely to damage the relationship you are trying to establish to ensure learning. Young people very quickly see a contradiction between a teacher who shouts in the classroom and one who, a few moments later, expects them to consider issues to do with spiritual, social and moral development. Instead:

- Train yourself to talk calmly, and be assertive but not aggressive.
- Avoid a public rebuke; talk to Steven in close proximity, or if possible away from his peers.
- Focus on the primary behaviour, not on secondary behaviour.
- Remind Steven of the school or classroom rule, making it clear that compliance is a requirement not a request: 'Remember the rule, Steven, no shouting. Thanks.'
- If possible require Steven to take responsibility for his behaviour by giving him a clear choice: 'Either sit down Steven and continue with your work or go to the "cool-off" room. It's your choice Steven.'
- Withdraw and avoid any further confrontation or rewarding Steven's aggressive behaviour with his wish for attention.
- If possible catch Steven being good and avoid sarcasm or irony: 'Thanks for putting your hand up Steven. How can I help?'
- Follow up after giving Steven an opportunity to cool off.
- Reward Steven's positive behaviour more than you reprimand him or punish his mistakes.
- Build in short rest periods or mini-breaks and allow all pupils, including Steven, to get out of their seats and have a stretch.

Steven may frequently drift off-task or task-refuse during his RE lessons. He may challenge the work or bait the RE teacher. For example, he may shout out, 'RE is rubbish!' or 'I hate RE.' It is easy for an RE teacher to take this personally and feel that they have to enter into a justification of the subject. In most cases this is not appropriate. If a student has serious uncertainties about what RE is about, this cannot be resolved with a two-minute discussion in the middle of a lesson. Steven may be involved in attention-seeking, and by indulging his desire, while you attempt to explain the virtues of RE, the likelihood is that he will employ similar behaviour the next time he wants a dose of attention. If Steven has a genuine concern about the role of RE in his education, the issue can be pursued with Steven after the lesson. Or perhaps the issue can be taken up on another occasion in a class discussion during which Steven would have an opportunity to more fully present his reservations. Instead, try to find a strategy for dealing with a challenge of this sort. For example:

- Remain calm, avoid taking the comment personally as a challenge to your role in the school. The likelihood is that Steven tells other subject teachers, 'Maths is boring!' or 'I really hate history.'
- Show that you are a human being and you acknowledge his feelings: 'Doing work you hate can be irritating, Steven.'
- Direct Steven back to the immediate task: 'Can you do the work, Steven? If not, I could give you some help, or I could find a partner for you to work with.'

Jenny Y7 – Down's syndrome (DS)

You will need to find out . . .

Initially Jenny's RE teacher will need to find out in what ways, and to what extent, she has general cognitive and learning difficulties which are typically associated with Down's syndrome. The degree of learning difficulty a person with DS may experience can vary enormously. It can range from mild to severe. This learning difficulty will lead to a development gap between Jenny and most of her peers. However, although this gap is likely to widen as she gets older, the evidence suggests that Jenny will nevertheless do better academically and socially working in an inclusive mainstream setting.

Jenny's cognitive and learning difficulties in RE may be due to a number of factors, all or only some of which Jenny may have. For example, Jenny may have a

- short-term auditory memory;
- speech and language impairment;
- hearing impairment;
- visual impairment;
- fine and gross motor skill impairment;
- thinking, reasoning and generalisation difficulties.

Within the school the most likely source of information about Jenny's specific learning difficulties will be Jenny herself. Jenny might well be very happy, indeed keen, to talk about what she can do and what she finds difficult. Listening to Jenny and giving her an opportunity to have a voice are important also for the development of self-esteem and social skills.

Apart from Jenny herself, other sources of valuable information and advice will include:

- Jenny's parents;
- the school's SENCO;
- Jenny's IEP or support plan;
- any teaching assistants that have experience of working with Jenny;
- the primary school transition information.

You should consider . . .

Regular meetings

In order to plan activities and support for Jenny during her RE lessons you should consider establishing regular meetings with the teaching assistant. The teaching assistant is likely to know Jenny well, but is unlikely to have much specialist knowledge of RE. Regular meetings with the TA are not undertaken as acts of mere professional courtesy. They are likely to greatly increase both the teacher's and the teaching assistant's effectiveness during lessons. However, it is important that the TA is not seen as belonging to Jenny, but is understood as belonging to the whole class. It is also important that Jenny's RE experience is not with the TA alone, but that in each lesson Jenny receives some personal interaction with the RE teacher as well.

Planning meetings with the RE teacher and the TA might be part of a wider schedule of meetings which also involve the SENCO, other curriculum class teachers and support staff. These meetings provide an opportunity to plan, feed back and monitor Jenny's progress generally.

Verbal instructions

You should also consider ensuring that Jenny understands what you say in the classroom. If Jenny has a short-term auditory memory, it is advisable to avoid long verbal instructions. Even relatively short verbal instructions or spoken information, if possible, should be divided up into more manageable chunks that enable Jenny to have time to assimilate what has been said.

In addition to the dividing up of spoken information, it may be helpful if Jenny can have such instructions or information repeated to her, or perhaps reinforced by the use of written or visual guidance.

Visual cues

The written word can help Jenny as it provides visual support, which reinforces the spoken word. For this reason Jenny is likely to find it helpful if you provide visual support in the form of flash cards, key words or picture cues. So, for example, the class may be asked to recall three things they remember about the Buddha from the previous lesson. Jenny is given three picture cues: the first shows the story of the boy Buddha and the wounded swan, a second shows the Buddha's enlightenment, and a third shows the story of the Buddha and the charging elephant.

Differentiation

Differentiated activities and resources, if they can be appropriately prepared, should also be considered. Handouts and worksheets continue to be a popular resource used by teachers of RE. Many teachers of RE find that available textbooks provide information which does not quite fit their learning intentions and so continue to prepare material of their own. However, handouts, if not prepared properly, can be a source of confusion and frustration. If thoughtfully differentiated they can be a valuable way of helping Jenny to make progress.

Any handouts or worksheets distributed to the class may in Jenny's case be in a larger font format. Although Jenny may be a good visual learner, she may have difficulty reading standard font sizes, like 11 or 12 points, due to visual impairment. The text may be simplified so as to contain the essential information. Particular attention should be given to ensuring a simple, clear layout and, if suitable, picture cues.

Jenny's homework should also be differentiated, particularly if she is set an assignment which requires writing. Not only might Jenny find that, because of her cognitive difficulties, understanding the homework could be a problem, but also poor muscle tone and loose joints (hypotonia) mean that her ability to write and the speed at which she writes are likely also to be affected.

A home–school book, in which Jenny's homework is written down for her, may prove to be helpful. It can also provide a valuable way in which Jenny's parents can give useful feedback and be more effectively involved in helping Jenny to make progress.

Seating arrangements

If Jenny does have both a visual and a hearing impairment, you may wish to encourage her to sit nearer the front of the class.

Some strategies you or the TA could try

The development gap between Jenny and most of her peers means that the activities and tasks set for her will be less challenging, but at the same time she should not find herself patronised by tasks which are trivial. What this might mean is that some pupils undertake tasks which require analysis, for example:

'Why do many Hindus worship using an image of a god?'

Or perhaps the task requires evaluation which is set in a challenging abstract context, for example:

'Does an image aid or hinder worship?'

Meanwhile, Jenny may still be following the same curriculum content, although her task requires mainly description rather analysis, for example:

'In the photo Ravi is worshipping the goddess Lakshmi. Describe what you can see.'

Jenny's work has to be carefully monitored, as it is all too easy to provide an over-diluted curriculum. It is quite possible that Jenny can express her own view or evaluate, as long as the question is asked in a context which is concrete and avoids too much abstraction, or if the question is put in an imaginative way, for example:

'Why is Ravi worshipping Lakshmi?' or 'If Ravi didn't worship Lakshmi, what would he miss?'

Jenny may be further aided in her response to such tasks by giving her more time to make a written response. Alternatively, she may be permitted to give a verbal response. It is important that you give her thinking time, so she can consider her answer, and sufficient time to say all that she wants to say. Jenny may also have speech difficulties. Because of this, her RE teacher should avoid anticipating her answer by finishing off her sentences for her.

Getting the level of challenge right for Jenny is particularly important. Differentiation in RE does not mean that while others are asked to think about the motives and purposes behind Hindu worship, Jenny is spending time copying and colouring in a picture of a Hindu god. Cloze activities may be a strategy that can be used, but if they involve merely slotting in one-word answers to complete a sentence, they are of dubious educational value. An RE curriculum should never become so diluted that Jenny is never asked to evaluate or offer her own opinion. Jenny may be helped to express her views using strategies such as:

* continuum line;
* multi-choice;
* writing frame.

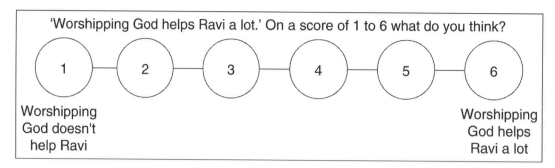

Figure 6.1 Continuum line.

'Ravi is worshipping Lakshmi because . . . ' Choose three which you agree with most.

it's Ravi's religion.	Lakshmi will bring Ravi good fortune.	Ravi likes Lakshmi.
it makes Ravi feel at peace inside.	Lakshmi reminds Ravi of God.	if he doesn't, Ravi thinks Lakshmi will be angry.
Lakshmi will make Ravi wealthy.	worshipping God is good for Ravi's soul.	worshipping helps Ravi become a better person.

Figure 6.2 Multi-choice.

My views about worship:

I think worship helps Ravi because. . . . .

. . . .

Worship is like . . . .

. . . .

An example of how worship can help Ravi is . . . .

. . . .

Some people think worship doesn't help people because . . . .

. . . .

But I don't agree with this view because . . . .

. . . .

Figure 6.3a Writing frame.

My views about worship:

I think worship does not help people because . . . .

. . . .

Some people believe that worship can help a person by . . . .

. . . .

An example of how some people think worship can help a person is . .

. . . .

But I don't agree with this because. . . . .

. . . .

Instead of worship I think . . . .

. . . .

Figure 6.3b Writing frame.

Such strategies should not be seen as achieving final outcomes but as spring-boards to further discussion and further refinement of thought. Jenny's ability to understand or form an opinion may be a good deal better than her ability to express her understanding or structure an argument. As a result, Jenny's cognitive and reasoning skills may easily be underestimated and so her progress held back.

As Jenny progresses into Key Stage 4, it is also important not to exclude her from the possibility of some form of national accreditation. If GCSE is judged to be inappropriate, other forms of accreditation should be explored, including Certificate of Achievement in Religious Studies and Entry Level qualifications.

Bhavini Y9 – visual impairment

You will need to find out . . .

There are many different degrees of visual impairment, ranging from low vision to blindness. Bhavini's RE teacher will need to find out the extent of Bhavini's visual impairment. A low-vision student, perhaps with the use of magnifica-tion equipment, may be able effectively to read print. Even if Bhavini is blind, the extent to which her impairment impedes her learning may vary depending on her background and training. For example, she may have a high degree of proficiency in Braille. Or she may have a well-developed auditory memory, which enables her to recall conversations or spoken information with a high level of accuracy.

If Bhavini does have some functional sight and is able to see print, you will need to find out what size print Bhavini is best able to see. It may be that a large print setting of 16–18 points suits Bhavini, or that she finds a particular font such as Arial visually much more comfortable than any other. If in the classroom you have available an interactive whiteboard, it may be that, following some research, Bhavini finds her visual discrimination is improved through the use of colour. For example, she may find it easier to see text in a particular colour, perhaps dark blue on yellow, rather than the standard default setting.

You will also need to find out if Bhavini finds it helpful to use relatively inexpensive equipment like a magnification lens, additional lighting or a sloping reading platform. It may be that Bhavini prefers to sit away from glaring light, for example by avoiding seats near a window. She may alternatively find it helpful to sit closer to the front of the classroom. It may also be the case that within the school Bhavini is familiar with certain working arrangements which she both prefers and finds helpful. For example, she may be used to working with a particular sighted partner or partners, or perhaps more generally she finds paired or group work greatly helps her learning. There may be established practices in the school which you would want to maintain. For example, Bhavini may usually leave the classroom a little early in order to give her extra time to get to her next lesson.

The source of much of this information will be available from the SENCO. However, it is also well worthwhile spending some time with Bhavini talking about her learning and how her learning can best be supported. This need not be a single, one-off meeting. Setting aside some time on a regular basis in order to speak to Bhavini can be of great help. Such regular meetings can

- provide useful information which can help inform how Bhavini can best be taught;
- provide useful feedback about what Bhavini has learnt and where additional support may be needed;
- engage Bhavini more fully in her own learning and so help her to take more responsibility for her learning.

You should consider . . .

Alternatives to using text

There are ways of conveying ideas and information in the RE classroom other than using text. Many RE lessons continue to make extensive use of reading and writing activities. The mistaken belief is that reading information from a book or a handout is an effective way of achieving learning. The value of the written word in the development of many of the world's religions has been immense, but the effectiveness of the written word in the RE classroom is greatly exaggerated.

That doesn't mean that the teacher of RE shouldn't continue to help Bhavini access the printed or the written word, for example by providing

- Bhavini with a reader or by offering to read the text for her; or
- tapes of text which Bhavini can listen to, using earphones.

However, it does mean that the teacher should be wary of excessive use of strategies which rely heavily on reading and writing in the RE classroom. Although many RE textbooks contain descriptions of religious rituals, festivals, beliefs and stories, reading such material often has very little appeal for young people, and so it is not surprising that the quality of recall or of understanding is often disappointing. Much more memorable strategies involve young people not in reading or writing, but instead in getting to their feet and physically participating or speaking, for example:

- a narrated reconstruction of what happens in a gurdwara during an Amrit service;
- playing games like dreidel and eating food such as cheese blintzes and potato latkes associated with the celebration of the festival of Hanukkah;
- preparing and performing a mock outside-TV broadcast on a topical issue of religious significance, e.g. performances of a play which gave religious offence are cancelled following a violent protest;
- organising a classroom debate on a topical religious issue, e.g. 'Should an employer be permitted to forbid the conspicuous wearing of symbols or clothing which shows religious affiliation at work?'

Bhavini will often be able to engage in such classroom activities unhindered by any difficulty she may have in seeing print or in writing text. By doing so, it is also more likely that all of the students will have a much stronger memory of the events or ideas being studied than would be achieved by the use of reading and writing strategies alone.

Generally increasing the opportunities for paired and group work may be of help to Bhavini, particularly if she finds it helpful to have a sighted partner to assist her with aspects of her work.

ICT support

You should also consider how ICT may be used to support Bhavini's learning; for example, voice recognition software would permit Bhavini to record her ideas and have the PC convert her spoken words into written text. Screen-reader software would make it possible for any text Bhavini might be researching to be accessed, as the text would be converted into a sound recording on a PC.

Some strategies you or the TA could try

The advantages of using kinaesthetic activities which involve simulating, in ways which are appropriate, rituals, ceremonies and festivals have already been outlined. However, difficult religious concepts and beliefs can also be made clearer to young people through the use of physical participation, which could be an effective learning strategy as much for Bhavini as for other students.

'Pass the Message'

This activity is designed to help young people understand the Islamic concept of revelation and the role of the prophets in Islamic thought. 'Pass the Message' involves dividing the class into two halves. One half invent a message. This message is passed to the other half of the class via an appointed messenger who repeats the message verbatim. Individuals in the receiving half of the class are asked to role-play ways in which a person may respond to the message over a period of time. For example, some mock the message, others ignore it, some write the message down verbatim, learn the message by heart and act on the message, while others attempt to memorise the message but distort the message over a period of time. Meanwhile, the other half of the class are given a similar task, but their messenger loosely extemporises the message.

'The Gauntlet and Candle'

'The Gauntlet and Candle' activity is intended to help young people to better understand the Jewish belief that the original Abrahamic–Mosaic concept of a single, just God has faced many historical threats to its survival. The survival of this concept of God, and indeed its widespread adoption, are thought to be a sign of its truth and of God acting in history. Most of the threats came from the powerful and clearly successful neighbouring empires of the Egyptians, the Assyrians, the Philistines, the Babylonians, the Greeks and the Romans. The class is divided into six groups, each group representing a neighbouring empire. Each group is then positioned in order to form a gauntlet or corridor. A volunteer carries a lighted non-extinguishable candle slowly through the gauntlet. Members of the gauntlet, as the candle passes, unsuccessfully attempt to blow out the candle. At the end of the gauntlet the candle is used to light two other candles to represent how the Abrahamic–Mosaic concept of God has become central to other traditions such as Islam and Christianity.

Tactile learning

Bhavini's learning can be supported by generally increasing tactile learning opportunities. So instead of merely being told about the Christian tradition of eating pancakes on Shrove Tuesday and making palm crosses in preparation for Palm Sunday, pupils are much more fully engaged, and likely to learn, if they actually eat a pancake and handle a palm cross.

Similarly, when it comes to using religious artefacts like a Buddhist prayer wheel, a Hindu puja bell, Christian incense, a Sikh kangha or a Sabbath spice box, such items should not be kept locked away in a display cabinet. Nor should they be held aloft for only sighted students to catch a glimpse of. Instead, following some discussion of how non-members of a religious tradition might show appropriate respect for the beliefs of others, such items should be passed around for pupils to hold and feel so that they acquire a multi-sensory memory of different faith traditions.

Additional strategies that can be undertaken include the following:

- If slides or images are being used, provide a description of those images.
- Make verbal instructions clear and avoid vague directional statements like 'over there', 'here' or 'this'.
- If you ask Bhavini a question, begin by using her name, e.g. 'Bhavini, what did your group find out about Islamic beliefs about stewardship?'
- Ensure that resources and materials like pencils, rulers and paper are stored in the same place so that Bhavini can exercise, where she can, independence in the classroom.

Susan Y10 – autistic spectrum disorder

You will need to find out . . .

You will need to find out the main characteristics and the severity of Susan's disorder. It is possible that Susan has been diagnosed with Asperger's syndrome. This might show itself in a complete lack of eye contact and an unwillingness to mix with other students during break and lunchtime. Nevertheless, Susan may have a highly focused intellect and be able to master a complex line of argument.

However, Susan's Asperger's might give rise to very different characteristics. The school's SENCO may be very familiar with the nature of Susan's Asperger and have either a very helpful IEP or detailed information about the way in which Susan's Asperger manifests itself. Susan's RE teacher needs to be aware of this information and use it as a basis for both the planning and the delivery of her RE lessons.

Susan may have a problem with motor control, resulting in poor handwriting. Because of this it may help Susan to be encouraged whenever possible to word-process her work.

You will also need to know if Susan has any history of unexpected or difficult behaviour. She may under some circumstances appear non-cooperative. She may appear to be deliberately disruptive, given on occasions to muttering or other verbal habits. Awareness of such characteristics can help prevent a teacher misconstruing Susan's behaviour and responding inappropriately.

You should consider . . .

A quiet area

Susan may feel more comfortable and be able to work better if a quiet, undisturbed area within the RE classroom can be arranged. Or the lighting may need to be adjusted in some way, or perhaps Susan is fixed on something which may seem inconsequential, like a squeaking window catch or a creaking chair, and can be resolved relatively easily.

Specialist interest

You should also consider if Susan has a particular area of specialist interest. For example, Susan may have a particular interest in animals, in the environment, in astronomy and space, or in the structure of buildings. It may be that her special interest can seem like a preoccupation. Nevertheless, it could be used as the basis for a special RE project which Susan may wish to pursue avidly. This need not be a solitary pursuit. With encouragement Susan may wish to work with a partner or to share her findings with others, or indeed with the rest of the class.

Need for routine

Susan may also have a need for routine, and any alterations in this routine may be unsettling. This does not mean that Susan cannot be involved in RE visits or that visiting speakers must be avoided. It may be helpful if other adults likely to meet Susan for the first time on such occasions are appropriately briefed. Susan's behaviour may seem odd, and an adult, on first acquaintance, might misconstrue the situation.

It may be that any changes in the routine need to be explained to Susan as fully as possible. Simply saying 'Next week we've got a visitor' may cause Susan to react with alarm. This can be avoided by providing much more information, for example: 'Next Wednesday Mrs Summers will talk to the class for about twenty minutes. Mrs Summers works for a charity called Oxfam. She will talk about trying to overcome hunger and poverty in the world. I will be in the classroom during the entire lesson.'

Susan's need for routine and order may cause you to consider how best to make the transition in RE from one topic to another, or from one religion to another. For example, having spent some weeks studying 'Christianity and Islam in the media', you may plan to change the topic entirely in order to make a study of 'Hinduism and the belief in Reincarnation'. Again, fully briefing Susan about the change, indeed explaining what topics will be studied, when they will be studied and for how long, can be of help to her and the pupils generally. Establishing clear boundaries between topics can also be of help. Making use of the natural breaks around fixed holidays can also be an advantage. However, visual reminders of a topic change, perhaps using colour or a separate display area, will help Susan and young people generally to organise and make sense of the information they are expected to learn.

Some strategies you or the TA could try

Susan may have an ability to recall factual information about religions but a weakness when understanding or abstract thought is required. For example, Susan may know the names and order of all the books in the Bible. However, if asked, 'Why is the Bible called a holy book?' Susan may appear bemused and offer only a literal response, 'Because it's holy.'

It would seem appropriate to tailor Susan's RE so that there is a focus on her strength, the learning of factual information about RE. However, such a programme of work would fall well short of what would normally be regarded as RE. Before deciding how Susan can best be taught RE, you should consider if Susan's weakness for understanding is because she has no real awareness of emotions and feelings, and it is this which leads her to make only factual or literal responses, or perhaps it is that Susan shows little emotion or feelings in her own life and this disguises more than might seem to be the case.

'What would you do?' activities

Susan might have little or nothing to say if asked, 'Why is the hajj important to Muslims?' The 'why' suggests an uncovering of the emotions and feelings of others which, expressed in this way, Susan has difficulty responding to. However, you should consider other strategies which Susan may find less inhibiting. If Susan were asked, 'What would you do?' rather than 'What are others feeling?' her response might be a good deal less stunted. For example, Susan might be able to make a much better response to the hajj task if she were asked: 'You are the manager of a small business. Four Muslims you employ ask for three weeks' leave so that they can go on hajj. It is a very busy time of the year for your business. What do you do?'

Symbolism and metaphor

Susan may experience difficulty understanding religious metaphor and symbolism, as in statements such as 'Heaven is up there', 'the Bread of Life', 'the Mother of the Book', 'the straight path', 'felt the Holy Spirit' and 'the House of God'. The religious concepts tied up in such statements are notoriously difficult to unravel. Susan may need help over a period of time, in order for her to slowly develop her understanding of this sort of language.

Explicit statements

When exploring the meaning of symbolic religious concepts, a useful strategy may be to invite students to attempt to pair up symbolic religious statements with statements which are clearly using words which are not intended to be understood in their everyday literal sense. For example, 'Heaven is up there' does not literally mean 'Heaven is several miles up', and 'The House of God' does not literally mean 'God is sitting inside the Ka'bah'. People with ASD often need very clear and explicit statements in order for them to understand. However, this does not form the end of the discussion but merely marks the beginning. Being explicit provides the basis on which further class discussion may take place, permitting a more sophisticated understanding to emerge.

Visual support

As is true of many people with ASD, Susan may be a strong visual thinker. Visual images and diagrams can be a valuable strategy for teaching abstract religious concepts. For example, a visual diagram might help Susan understand the Hindu belief that both Rama and Krishna and others are incarnations of the Hindu god Vishnu.

Examination preparation

If Susan is working towards an exam leading to a national accreditation, careful preparation is needed:

- Susan will need to be told as soon as possible the date, time and length of the examination.
- Susan should be given a good idea of how many other people will be in the room or hall taking the exam and who will be adjudicating.
- The seating arrangements and a plan of where she will be sitting may help Susan cope with any sense of anxiety.
- If Susan is hypersensitive to extraneous sounds, like the squeaky shoes of the invigilator or the buzz from fluorescent lights, she may be helped by awareness of relaxation techniques or more directly, if permitted, by the use of earplugs.
- It may be advisable for Susan to be allowed to enter early into the space in which the exam will take place as she may need time to adjust to the new environment. It is not unknown for students with ASD to have to touch all of the walls of an examination room before they felt sufficiently comfortable to sit the exam.

Discuss external exam arrangements with the SENCO and assessment/examinations coordinator well in advance of the actual exam; special arrangements and concessions may be possible.

Appendix 1 SEND legislation

The Children and Families Act: a different landscape

The Children and Families Act 2014 introduced radical changes to the requirements placed on both schools and teachers regarding the education and inclusion of pupils with special educational needs and disabilities. Part 3 of the Act heralded the first major revision of the SEND framework for thirty years and not only introduced a new system to help children with special educational needs and disabilities but importantly also shapes how education, health and social care professionals should work in partnership with children, young people and their families.

The reforms introduced a system designed around the needs of children and young people that will support them potentially from birth up to the age of 25. This extension into adulthood is designed to ensure that young people experience a smooth transition across all services as they move from school into further education, training and employment. The reforms give particular emphasis to preparing children and young people for adulthood from the earliest years. This means enabling children to be involved at as young an age as possible in all decisions relating to their learning, therapy, medical treatment and support from social care. The result of this preparation should be that when young people reach the age of 16, they are able to be full and active participants in all important decisions about their life.

> There is now an important distinction made between a child and a young person. The Act gives significant new rights directly to young people when they are over compulsory school age but under the age of 25. Under the Act, a child becomes a young person after the last day of summer term during the academic year in which he or she turns 16. This is subject to a young person 'having capacity' to take a decision under the Mental Capacity Act 2005.

Throughout this book the term 'pupils with special educational needs and disabilities (SEND)' is used. A pupil has special educational needs if he or she:

- has a significantly greater difficulty in learning than the majority of others of the same age; or
- has a disability which prevents or hinders him or her from making use of facilities of a kind generally provided for others of the same age in mainstream schools or mainstream Post-16 institutions.

(SEND Code of Practice 2015, p. 15)

The term 'parent' is used throughout and is intended to cover any additional main care-givers.

Section 19 principles

Central to Part 3 of the Children and Families Act 2014 is Section 19. This section sets out the principles underpinning the legislation and outlines what is expected of local authorities, schools, health and social care services in their work with children and young people with SEND and their families. Section 19 states:

In exercising a function under this Part in the case of a child or young person, a local authority in England must have regard to the following matters in particular –

a) the views, wishes and feelings of the child and his or her parent, or the young person;
b) the importance of the child and his or her parent, or the young person, participating as fully as possible in decisions relating to the exercise of the function concerned;
c) the importance of the child and his or her parent, or the young person, being provided with the information and support necessary to enable participation in those decisions;
d) the need to support the child and his or her parent, or the young person, in order to facilitate the development of the child or young person and to help him or her achieve the best possible educational and other outcomes.

(SEND Code of Practice 2015, 1.1, p. 19)

It is rare to see the word 'feelings' used in legislation and Part A of Section 19 is particularly significant because it goes beyond an expectation of schools consulting parents towards a situation where the views of parents, children and young people have equal status with those of professionals. This does not mean that parents will necessarily always be given what they want, nor that parents will be able to dictate teaching strategies or medical treatments. What it does mean is that parents, pupils and professionals each bring their varying knowledge, experience and expertise to decisions for the benefit – and best possible outcomes – of the child or young person.

The expectations of Section 19 do not in any way diminish the importance of the teacher's pedagogy and teaching skill, rather they ally that professional expertise with the parents' deep knowledge of their own child in the context of their unique family and the pupils' own special interests and motivators. When all these skills, experience and understanding are combined, a firm foundation is created on which to build a unique learning programme and, perhaps most importantly, to develop real trust across all parties.

Part C of Section 19 issues a new challenge to schools in that there is a clear expectation not only that parents and pupils will be invited to participate but also that they should be supported to do so. This will certainly involve the provision of relevant information to parents but schools could also consider providing other forms of support: both practical support, such as helping with translation services, or even transport to attend important meetings, and emotional support, such as advocacy or pre-meetings to prepare parents and pupils to take a full part in all decisions. Many parents will need only a minimal level of additional support, but others – especially those often portrayed as 'hard to reach' – may require considerably more. What, for example, should a school do when parents do not attend an annual review meeting? In the past, these reviews often went ahead regardless, without any investigation of the reasons why the parents would not or could not attend. Here again Section 19 raises the bar of expectations and schools will need to find new ways to involve parents and to ensure they are full participants in decisions about their child.

Key questions:

- Do you know the wishes and feelings about education of your pupils with SEND and their parents? If not, how can you find out?
- What could you and others in your subject/departmental team do to integrate this information into your planning for and delivery of teaching and learning?
- What more could you do to reach out to parents who may be anxious about or unwilling to engage with school?

The SEND Code of Practice

As the quotation at the start of this chapter makes clear, SEND provision is provision that is additional to or different from the high-quality, differentiated and personalised teaching to which all pupils are entitled. A school's first response to a pupil falling behind his or her peers should be to evaluate the quality of teaching and learning the pupil currently receives in all subjects. The pupil should be identified as having SEND only when the school is confident that all teaching is well differentiated and personalised to meet that individual pupil's needs.

Once a pupil is identified as having SEND, schools are required to do whatever they can to remove any barriers to learning and to put in place effective provision, or 'SEND support'. This support must enable pupils with SEND to achieve the best possible outcomes.

Most schools and academies welcome pupils with a range of vulnerabilities, including special educational needs and disabilities, but may hesitate about including those with significant or complex needs. The reasons behind this reluctance are often a lack of expertise in an area of need, worries about behaviour and, most commonly expressed, concerns about the impact of that pupil's needs on the education of others.

The SEND Code of Practice is very clear that where the parent of a pupil with an education, health, and care plan (EHC plan) makes a request for a particular school, the local authority *must* comply with that preference and name the school in the plan unless:

- it would be unsuitable for the age, ability, aptitude or SEND of the child or young person, or
- the attendance of the child or young person there would be incompatible with the efficient education of others, or the efficient use of resources.

(DfE 2015, 9.79, p. 172)

Legally, schools cannot refuse to admit a pupil who does not have an EHC plan because they do not feel able to cater for his or her needs, or because the pupil does not have an EHC plan.

Outcomes

An outcome is the benefit or difference made for an individual as result of the educational or training intervention provided. Outcomes are written from the perspective of the pupil rather than that of a service and should identify what the provision is intended to achieve. For example, do you think the following is an outcome for a pupil in Year 7 with literacy difficulties?

For the next 10 weeks Jake will work on an online literacy program for twenty minutes three times each week.

It may be specific and measurable; it is achievable and realistic; and it is time targeted, so it is 'SMART' but it isn't an outcome. What is described here is provision, i.e. the intervention that the school will use to help Jake to make accelerated progress.

Outcomes are intended to look forward to the end of the next stage or phase of education, usually two or three years hence. Teachers will, of course, set short-term targets covering between six and twelve weeks, and education and health Plans will also include interim objectives to be discussed at annual reviews. So, what would be an outcome for Jake?

> By the end of Year 9, Jake will be able to read and understand the textbooks for his chosen GCSE courses.

The online literacy course would then form a part of the package of provision to enable Jake to achieve this outcome.

By using an outcomes-focused approach, schools can ensure that the special educational provision offered to a pupil is focused on a clear identification of his or her strengths and needs, and on a clear understanding of what has worked well in the past, and what needs to be improved.

The graduated approach

The SEND Code of Practice describes SEND support as a cyclical process of assess, plan, do and review that is known as the 'graduated approach'. This cycle is already commonly used in schools, and for pupils with SEND it is intended to be much more than a token, in-house process. Rather it should be a powerful mechanism for reflection and evaluation of the impact of SEND provision. Through the four-part cycle, decisions and actions are revisited, refined and revised. This then leads to a deeper understanding of an individual pupil's needs whilst also offering an insight into the effectiveness of the school's overall provision for pupils with SEND. The graduated approach offers the school, the pupil and his or her parents a growing understanding of needs and of what provision the pupil requires to enable him or her to make good progress and secure good outcomes. Through successive cycles, the graduated approach draws on increasingly specialist expertise, assessments and approaches, and more frequent reviews. This structured process gives teachers the information they need to match specific, evidence-based interventions to pupils' individual needs.

Evidence-based interventions

In recent years, a number of universities and other research organisations have produced evidence about the efficacy of a range of different interventions for vulnerable pupils and pupils with SEND. Most notable among this research is that sponsored by the Education Endowment Fund that offers schools valid data on the impact of interventions and the optimal conditions for their use. Other important sources of information about evidence based interventions for specific areas of need are the Communication Trust 'What Works?' website and 'Interventions for Literacy' from the SpLD/Dyslexia Trust. Both sites offer transparent and clear information for professionals and parents to support joint decisions about provision.

The Equality Act 2010

Sitting alongside the Children and Families Act 2014, the requirements of the Equality Act 2010 remain firmly in place. This is especially important because many children and young people who have SEND may also have a disability under the Equality Act. The definition of disability in the Equality Act is that the child or young person has 'a physical or mental impairment which has a long-term and substantial adverse effect on a person's ability to carry out normal day-to-day activities'. 'Long-term' is defined as lasting or being likely to last for 'a year or more', and 'substantial' is defined as 'more than minor or trivial'. The definition includes sensory impairments such as those affecting sight or hearing, and, just as crucially for schools, children with long-term health conditions such as asthma, diabetes, epilepsy and cancer.

As the SEND Code of Practice (DfE 2015, p. 16) states, the definition for disability provides a relatively low threshold and includes many more children than schools may realise. Children and young people with some conditions do not necessarily have SEND, but there is often a significant overlap between disabled children and young people and those with SEND. Where a disabled child or young person requires special educational provision, they will also be covered by the SEND duties.

The Equality Act applies to all schools, including academies and free schools, university technical colleges and studio schools, and also further education colleges and sixth form colleges – even where the school or college has no disabled pupils currently on roll. This is because the duties under the Equality Act are anticipatory in that they cover not only current pupils but also prospective ones. The expectation is that all schools will be reviewing accessibility continually and making reasonable adjustments in order to improve access for disabled pupils. When thinking about disabled access, the first thing that school leaders usually consider is physical access, such as wheelchair access, lifts and ramps. But physical access is only part of the requirement of the Equality Act and often is the simplest to improve. Your school's accessibility plan for disabled pupils must address all of three elements of planned improvements in access:

1. physical improvements to increase access to education and associated services;
2. improvements in access to the curriculum;
3. improvements in the provision of information for disabled pupils in a range of formats.

Improvements in access to the curriculum are often a harder nut to crack as they involve all departments and all teachers looking closely at their teaching and learning strategies and evaluating how effectively these meet the needs of disabled pupils. Often, relatively minor amendments to the curriculum or teaching approaches can lead to major improvements in access for disabled pupils, and these often have a positive impact on the education of all pupils. For example, one school installed a Soundfield amplification system in a number of classrooms because a pupil with a hearing loss had joined the school. The following year, the cohort of Year 7 pupils had particularly poor speaking and listening skills and it was noticed that they were more engaged in learning when they were taught in the rooms with the Soundfield system. This led to improvements in progress for the whole cohort and significantly reduced the level of disruption and off-task behaviours in those classes.

Schools also have wider duties under the Equality Act to prevent discrimination, to promote equality of opportunity, and to foster good relations. These duties should inform all aspects of school improvement planning from curriculum design through to anti-bullying policies and practice.

Significantly, a pupil's underachievement or behaviour difficulties might relate to an underlying physical or mental impairment which could be covered by the Equality Act. A school would have difficulty claiming not to have known about a disability if a pupil's behaviour or underachievement suggested he or she might be disabled.

Each pupil is different and will respond to situations in his or her unique way, so a disability should be considered in the context of the child as an individual. The 'social model' of disability sees the environment as the primary disabling factor, as opposed to the 'medical model' that focuses on the individual child's needs and difficulties. School activities and environments should be considered in the light of possible barriers to learning or participation.

What are the corridors like during the changeover between lessons?

Are they calm and orderly, or are they noisy, crowded and chaotic? If the latter, what impact do you think this would have on a pupil with autism who has sensory issues with sound and touch? All too often, such scenarios can lead to a pupil with SEND becoming very anxious, perhaps lashing out in fear. The pupil is then usually punished. Rather than blaming the pupil, the school should improve the environment so that such situations are avoided.

Appendix 2 Departmental policy

Whether the practice in your school is to have separate SEND policies for each department or to embed the information on SEND in your whole-school inclusion or teaching and learning policies, the processes and information detailed below will still be relevant.

Good practice for pupils with SEN and disabilities is good practice for all pupils, especially those who are 'vulnerable' to underachievement. **Vulnerable groups** may include looked-after children (LAC), pupils for whom English is an additional language (EAL), pupils from minority ethnic groups, young carers, and pupils known to be eligible for free school meals. Be especially aware of those pupils with SEND who face one or more additional vulnerabilities and for whom effective support might need to go beyond help in the classroom.

It is crucial that your departmental or faculty policy describes a strategy for meeting pupils' special educational needs within your particular curricular area. The policy should set the scene for any visitor, from supply staff to inspectors, and make a valuable contribution to the department handbook. The process of developing a departmental SEND policy offers the opportunity to clarify and evaluate current thinking and practice within the RE team and to establish a consistent approach.

The SEND policy for your department is a significant document in terms of the leadership and management of your subject. The preparation or review of the policy should be led by a senior manager within the team because that person needs to have sufficient status to be able to influence subsequent practice and training across the department. Policy and practice in SEND provision go much wider than individual pupils' needs; they will be influenced by, and will have an impact on, other major aspects such as:

- the school ethos and values system;
- teaching and learning;
- whole-school behaviour management;

- the deployment of staff; and, perhaps most significantly,
- leadership and management.

What should a departmental policy contain?

The policy should:

- clarify the responsibilities of all staff;
- identify any colleagues who have had specialist training and/or have in-depth knowledge and experience of SEND provision;
- describe the curriculum on offer and how it can be differentiated (including signposts to resources);
- specify the process for putting in place special exam arrangements;
- outline arrangements for assessing and reporting;
- offer guidance to teachers on how to work effectively with support staff.

The starting points for your departmental SEND policy will be the whole-school SEND policy and the SEND Information Report that, under the Children and Families Act 2014, all schools are required to publish. Each subject department's own SEND policy should then 'flesh out' the detail in a way that describes how things will work in practice. Writing the policy needs to be much more than a paper exercise completed merely to satisfy the senior management team and Ofsted inspectors. Rather, it is an opportunity for your staff to come together as a team to create a framework for teaching RE in a way that makes your subject accessible not only to pupils with special educational needs and disabilities, but to all pupils in the school.

Who should be involved in developing your SEND policy?

The job of developing or reviewing your policy will be made much easier if you involve others in the task. Other people who will be able to offer support and guidance include:

- the school SEND governor;
- the SENCO or other school leader with responsibility for SEND;
- your support staff, including teaching assistants and technicians;
- the school data manager, who will be able to offer information about the attainment and progress of different groups;
- outside experts from your local authority, academy chain or other schools;
- parents of pupils with SEND;
- pupils themselves – both with and without SEND.

Bringing together a range of views and information will enable you to develop a policy that is compliant with the letter *and* principle of the legislation, that is relevant to the context of your school, and that is useful in guiding practice and improving outcomes for all pupils.

The role of parents in developing your departmental SEND policy

As outlined in Appendix 1, Section 19 of the Children and Families Act 2014 raises the bar of expectations about how parents should be involved in and influence the work of schools. Not only is it best practice to involve parents of pupils with SEND in the development of policy, but it will also help in 'getting it right' for both pupils and staff. There are a number of ways, both formal and informal, to find out the views of parents to inform policy writing, including:

- a focus group;
- a coffee morning/drop-in;
- a questionnaire/online survey;
- a phone survey of a sample of parents.

Parents will often respond more readily if the request for feedback or the invitation to attend a meeting comes from their son or daughter.

Where to start when writing a policy

An audit can act as a starting point for reviewing current policy on SEND or writing a new policy. This will involve gathering information and reviewing current practice with regard to pupils with SEND and is best completed by the whole department, preferably with some input from the SENCO or another member of staff with responsibility for SEND within the school. An audit carried out by the whole department provides a valuable opportunity for professional development so long as it is seen as an exercise in sharing good practice and encourages joint planning. It may also facilitate your department's contribution to the school provision map. But before embarking on an audit, it is worth investing some time in a departmental meeting, or ideally a training day, to raise awareness of the legislation around special educational needs and disabilities and to establish a shared philosophy across your department.

The following headings may be useful when you are establishing your departmental policy:

General statement of compliance

- What is the overarching aim of the policy? What outcomes do you want to achieve for pupils with SEND?
- How are you complying with legislation and guidance?

- What does the school SEND Information Report say about teaching and learning and provision for pupils with SEND?

Definition of SEND

- What does SEND mean?
- What are the areas of need and the categories used in the Code of Practice?
- Are there any special implications for your subject area?

Provision for staff within the department

- Who has responsibility for SEND within the department?
- What information about pupils' SEND is held, where is it stored and how is it shared?
- How can staff access additional resources, information and training?
- What assessments are available for teachers in your department to support accurate identification of SEND?

Provision for pupils with SEND

- How are pupils' special educational needs identified, assessed and monitored in the department?
- How do members of the department contribute to individual learning plans, meetings with parents and reviews?
- What criteria are used for organising teaching groups?
- What additional support is available to pupils with SEND from teachers and support staff?
- What adjustments are made for pupils with special educational needs and/ or disabilities in lessons and homework?
- How do we use information about pupils' abilities in reading, writing, speaking and listening when planning lessons and homework?
- What alternative courses are available for pupils with SEND?
- What special arrangements are made for internal and external examinations?
- What guidance is available for working effectively with support staff?

Resources and learning materials

- Is any specialist equipment used in the department?
- How are differentiated resources developed? What criteria do we use (e.g. literacy levels)?
- Where are resources stored and are they accessible for both staff and pupils?

Staff qualifications and continuing professional development (CPD)

- What qualifications and experience do the members of the department have? (One department which carried out this exercise found that they had an expert in EAL and ex-SEND teaching assistant in the team.)
- What training has already taken place, and when? What impact did that training have on teaching and learning, and progress for pupils with SEND?
- How is training planned? What criteria are used to identify training needs?
- What account of SEND is taken when new training opportunities are proposed?
- Is a record kept of training completed and ongoing training needs?

Monitoring and reviewing the policy

- How will the policy be monitored?
- Who will lead the monitoring?
- When will the policy be reviewed?

The content of a departmental SEND policy

This section offers more information on what a SEND policy might include, with examples of statements for you to amend for the context of your school.

General statement with reference to the school's SEND policy

Under the Children and Families act 2014, all schools must have a SEND policy and publish a SEND Information Report. The SEND policy will set out the basic information on the school's SEND provision and how the school identifies, assesses and provides for pupils with SEND, including information on staffing and working in partnership with parents and other professionals. Any departmental policy needs to have reference to the school SEND policy and should reflect the contents of the SEND Information Report.

Example

All members of the department will ensure that the needs of all pupils with SEND are met, according to the aims of the school and its SEND policy.

Definition of SEND

The definition of SEND in the SEND Code of Practice is exactly the same as in the 2002 Code of Practice (see Appendix 1). It is useful to insert in your policy the four broad areas of SEND identified in the SEND Code of Practice, but remember that the four areas give only an overview of the range of needs that should be planned for by schools; pupils' needs rarely fit neatly into one area of need.

Table A2.1 The four broad areas of SEND

Communication and interaction	Cognition and learning	Social, emotional and mental health difficulties	Sensory and/or physical needs
Speech, language and communication needs (SLCN)	Specific learning difficulties (SpLD)	Mental health difficulties such as anxiety or depression, self-harming, substance abuse or eating disorders	Vision impairment (VI)
Asperger's syndrome and autism (ASD)	Moderate learning difficulties (MLD)		Hearing impairment (HI)
	Severe learning difficulties (SLD)		Multi-sensory impairment (MSI)
	Profound and multiple learning difficulties (PMLD)	Attention deficit disorders, attention deficit hyperactivity disorder or attachment disorder	Physical disability (PD)

Provision for staff within the department

In many schools, each department nominates a member of staff to have responsibility and oversight for SEND provision (with or without remuneration). This can be very effective where there is a system of regular liaison between department SEND representatives and the SENCO in the form of meetings or paper/email communications or both.

The responsibilities of this post may include:

- liaison between the department and the SENCO;
- monitoring the progress of and outcomes for pupils with SEND, e.g. identifying attainment gaps between pupils with SEND and their peers;
- attending any liaison meetings and providing feedback to colleagues;
- attending and contributing to training;
- maintaining departmental SEND information and records;
- representing the needs of pupils with SEND at departmental level;

- liaising with parents of pupils with SEND;
- gathering feedback from pupils with SEND on the impact of teaching and support strategies on their learning and well-being.

The post can be seen as a valuable development opportunity for staff, and the name of this person should be included in the policy. However, where responsibility for SEND is given to a relatively junior member of the team, there must be support and supervision from the head of the department to ensure that the needs of pupils with SEND have sufficient prominence in both policy and practice.

How members of the department raise concerns about pupils with SEND can be included in this section. Concerns may be raised at specified departmental meetings before referral to the SENCO. The department's first response to concerns about a pupil's progress should be to evaluate the quality of the teaching and learning experienced by the pupil in your subject lessons. Only when all members of the department team are confident that the teaching in those lessons is of a high quality, and is sufficiently differentiated to meet the pupil's individual needs, should SEND support be considered.

It is good practice to ask the SENCO for advice and guidance on how to improve the identification of needs and appropriate teaching strategies.

Reference to working with support staff will include a commitment to effective planning and communication between teachers and teaching assistants. There may also be information on how support staff will be involved in meetings, developing resources and lesson planning.

A reference to the list of pupils with SEND and other relevant information will also be included in this section, along with a note about confidentiality.

Example

The member of staff with responsibility for overseeing the provision of SEND within the department will attend liaison meetings and subsequently give feedback to the other members of the department. S/he will maintain the department's SEND file, attend and/or organise appropriate training and disseminate this to all departmental staff. All information will be treated with confidentiality.

Provision for pupils with SEND

It is the responsibility of all staff to know which pupils have been identified with SEND and, additionally, to identify any pupils experiencing difficulties. Pupils with SEND may be identified by staff within the department in a variety of ways; these may be listed and could include:

- observation in lessons;
- assessment of class work;
- homework tasks;
- end of module tests;
- progress checks;
- annual examinations;
- reports.

Setting out how pupils with SEND are grouped within the RE department may include specifying the criteria used, the philosophy behind the process and details about reviewing the composition of groups. Monitoring arrangements and details of how pupils can move between groups should also be set out. Information collected may include:

- end-of-Key-Stage results;
- baseline data assessed on entry to the school;
- departmental assessments (being clear about the precise evidence on which they are based);
- reading scores;
- advice from pastoral staff;
- discussion with staff in the SEND department;
- information provided in provision maps and one-page profiles.

Example

Pupils are grouped according to ability, using information from:

- CAT scores;
- SATs information;
- termly tests;
- teacher assessments/observations.

Pupils may move between groups when . . .

The exercise of writing or reviewing your SEND policy is an ideal opportunity to discuss the impact of grouping on academic and social outcomes for pupils. (Bear in mind that the Code of Practice includes a specific duty that 'schools must ensure that pupils with SEN engage in the activities of the school alongside pupils who do not have SEN' (DfE 2015, 6.2, p. 92).

We need to be careful in RE that, when grouping pupils, we are not bound solely by measures in reading and writing, but also take into account reasoning and oral language abilities. It is vital that social issues are also taken into consideration if pupils are to be able to learn effectively. Having a complement of pupils with good oral ability will lift the attitude and attainment of everybody within a group.

Special examination arrangements need to be considered for both external and internal examinations. How, when and with whom these arrangements will be discussed should be clarified. Reference to the SENCO and the requirements of the examination boards should be taken into account.

Here is a good place also to put a statement about the school behaviour policy and any rewards and sanctions, and how the department will make any necessary adjustments to meet the needs of pupils with SEND.

Example

The staff in the RE department will aim to support pupils with SEND to achieve the best possible outcomes. They will do this by supporting pupils to achieve their individual targets as specified in their individual learning plans, and will provide feedback for progress reviews. Pupils with SEND will be included in the departmental monitoring system used for all pupils.

Resources and learning materials

The departmental policy needs to identify what differentiated materials are available, where they are kept and how new resources will be sourced. This section could include a statement about working with support staff and TAs to develop resources or access specialist resources as needed, while making it clear that the responsibility for differentiating learning materials lies squarely with the subject teacher. Teaching strategies may also be identified if appropriate.

> **Example**
>
> The department will provide suitably differentiated materials and, where appropriate, specialist resources to meet the needs of pupils with SEND. Alternative courses and examinations will be made available, where appropriate, for individual pupils. Support staff will be provided with curriculum information in advance of lessons and will be involved in lesson planning. A list of resources is available in the department handbook.

Staff qualifications and continuing professional development

It is important to recognise and record the qualifications and special skills gained by staff within the department (teachers and support staff). Training can include not only external courses but also in-house training opportunities such as observing other staff, working alongside colleagues to produce materials, and visiting other schools to see good practice. This information should also highlight any areas where there is little or no expertise or experience within the department and where additional training needs to be sought. For example, autism is no longer a low-incidence area of need and it is highly likely that all educational professionals will encounter and work with pupils on the autistic spectrum throughout their careers, so all teachers and support staff should have at least a good awareness of how they can adapt their teaching and support for these pupils.

> **Example**
>
> A record of training undertaken, specialist skills and training required will be kept in the department handbook. Requests for training will be considered in line with the department and school improvement plan.

Monitoring and reviewing the policy

To be effective, all policies must be monitored and reviewed regularly. This can be planned as part of the yearly cycle. The responsibility for the monitoring can rest with the head of department but will have more effect if supported by someone from a different department acting as a critical friend. This could be the SENCO or a member of the senior management team in the school.

> **Example**
>
> The departmental SEND policy will be monitored by the head of department on a planned annual basis, with advice being sought from the SENCO as part of the three-yearly review process.

Conclusion

Creating a departmental SEND policy should be a developmental activity that will improve teaching and learning for all pupils, but especially for those who are vulnerable to underachievement. The policy should be a working document that will evolve and change over time; it is there to challenge current practice and to encourage improvement for both pupils and staff. If departmental staff work together to create the policy, they will have ownership of it; it will have true meaning and be effective in clarifying good practice.

An example of a departmental policy for you to amend is available on the website: www.routledge.com/9781138683778.

Appendix 3 Types of SEND

Introduction

This appendix is a starting point for information on the special educational needs most frequently encountered in mainstream schools. It describes the main characteristics of each area of special educational need and disability (SEND) with practical ideas for use in RE lessons, and contacts for further information.

There is a measure of repetition, as some strategies prove to be effective with a whole range of pupils (and often with those who have no identified SEND). However, the layout enables readers an 'at a glance' reminder of effective approaches and facilitates copying for colleagues and TAs.

The SEND Code of Practice (DfE 2015) outlines four broad areas of need. These are:

- communication and interaction;
- cognition and learning;
- social, emotional and mental health difficulties;
- sensory and/or physical needs.

These broad areas are not exclusive and pupils may have needs that cut across some or all of them. Equally, pupils' difficulties and needs will change over time. The terms used in this chapter are helpful when reviewing and monitoring special educational provision, but pupils' individual talents and interests are just as important as their disability or special educational need. Because of this, specific terms or labels need to be used with care in discussion with parents, pupils or other professionals. Unless a pupil has a firm diagnosis, and parents and pupil understand the implications of that diagnosis, it is more appropriate to describe the features of the special educational need rather than use the label. For example, a teacher might describe a pupil's spelling difficulties but not use the term 'dyslexic'.

There is a continuum of need within each of the special educational needs and disabilities listed here. Some pupils will be affected more than others and show fewer or more of the characteristics described.

Pupils with other, less common special educational needs may be included in some schools, and additional information on these conditions may be found in a variety of sources. These include the school SENCO, local authority support services, educational psychologists and online information, for example on the Nasen SEND Gateway and disability charity websites such as those of Mencap, CAF or I CAN, the children's communication charity.

Further information

www.nasen.org.uk
www.mencap.org.uk
www.cafamily.org.uk
www.ican.org.uk

Attention deficit disorder (with or without hyperactivity) ADD/ADHD

Attention deficit hyperactivity disorder is one of the most common childhood disorders and can continue through adolescence and adulthood. ADHD can occur in pupils of any intellectual ability and may also cause additional problems, such as sleep and anxiety disorders. The features of ADHD usually diminish with age, but many individuals who are diagnosed with the condition at a young age will continue to experience problems in adulthood.

Main characteristics

- short attention span or easily distracted by noise and movement
- difficulty in following instructions and completing tasks
- difficulty in listening to and processing verbal instructions
- restlessness, inability to keep still causing frequent fidgeting
- difficulty with moderating behaviour such as constant talking, interrupting and calling out
- difficulty in waiting or taking turns
- impulsivity – acting without thinking about consequences

How can the RE teacher help?

- Make eye contact and use the pupil's name when speaking to him.
- Keep instructions simple – the one sentence rule.
- Provide clear written instructions.
- Position the pupil away from obvious distractions, e.g. windows, computer screens.
- Provide clear routines and rules, and rehearse them regularly.
- Encourage the pupil to repeat instructions (to you or TA) before starting work.
- Tell the pupil when to begin a task.
- Give two choices – avoid the option of the pupil saying 'no', e.g. 'Do you want to write in blue or black pen?'
- Give advanced warning when something is about to happen. Signal a change or finish with a time, e.g. 'In two minutes I need you (pupil name) to . . .'
- Give specific praise – catch him being good, give attention for positive behaviour.
- Give the pupil responsibilities so that others can see him in a positive light and he develops a positive self-image.

Further information

ADDISS   020 8952 2800   www.addiss.co.uk
ADHD Foundation   0151 237 2661   www.adhdfoundation.org.uk
Young Minds   020 7089 5050   www.youngminds.org.uk
Autism (ASD)

Asperger syndrome

Asperger syndrome is a type of autism. People with Asperger syndrome do not have 'learning difficulties' as such, but they do have difficulties associated with being on the autistic spectrum. They often want to make friends but do not understand the complex rules of social interaction. They may have impaired fine and gross motor skills, with writing being a particular problem. Boys are more likely to be affected – with the ratio being 10:1 boys to girls. Because they appear 'odd' and naive, these pupils are particularly vulnerable to bullying.

Main characteristics

- **Social interaction**
  Pupils with Asperger syndrome want friends but have not developed the strategies necessary for making and sustaining meaningful friendships. They find it very difficult to learn social norms and to pick up on social cues. Social situations, such as assemblies and less formal lessons, can cause great anxiety.

- **Social communication**
  Pupils have appropriate spoken language but tend to sound formal and pedantic, using limited expression and possibly an unusual tone of voice. They have difficulty using and understanding non-verbal language such as facial expression, gesture, body language and eye contact. They may have a literal understanding of language and do not grasp implied meanings.

- **Social imagination**
  Pupils with Asperger syndrome need structured environments, and to have routines they understand and can anticipate. They may excel at learning facts but have difficulty understanding abstract concepts and in generalising information and skills. They often have all-consuming special interests.

How can the RE teacher help?

- Liaise closely with parents, especially over homework.
- Create as calm a classroom environment as possible.
- Allow to sit in the same place for each lesson.
- Set up a 'work buddy' system for your lessons.
- Provide additional visual cues in class, such as visual timetables and task activity lists.
- Give the pupil time to process questions and respond.
- Make sure pupils understand what you expect of them.
- Offer alternatives to handwriting for recording work.
- Prepare pupils for changes to routines well in advance.

- Give written homework instructions.
- Have your own class rules and apply them consistently.

Further information

The National Autistic Society   020 7833 2299   www.autism.org.uk/about/what-is/asperger.aspx

Autism spectrum disorder (ASD)

Autism is a developmental disability that affects how a person communicates with, and relates to, other people. It also affects how they make sense of the world around them. It is often referred to as a spectrum or ASD which means that, while all people with autism share certain difficulties, the condition may affect them in different ways. Pupils with ASD cover the full range of academic ability and the severity of the disability varies widely. Some pupils also have learning disabilities or other difficulties, such as dyslexia. Four times as many boys as girls are diagnosed with an ASD.

Main characteristics

- **Social interaction**
  Pupils with ASD find it difficult to understand social behaviour and this affects their ability to interact with others. They do not always understand social contexts. They may experience high levels of stress and anxiety in settings that do not meet their needs or when routines are changed. This can lead to inappropriate behaviour.

- **Social communication**
  Understanding and use of non-verbal and verbal communication are impaired. Pupils with an ASD have difficulty understanding the communication of others and in developing effective communication themselves. They may have a literal understanding of language. Many are delayed in learning to speak, and some people with ASD never develop speech at all.

- **Social imagination and flexibility of thought**
  Pupils with an ASD have difficulty in thinking and behaving flexibly which may result in restricted, obsessional or repetitive activities. They are often more interested in objects than people, and have intense interests in such things as trains and vacuum cleaners. Pupils work best when they have a routine. Unexpected changes in those routines will cause distress.

Some pupils with autistic spectrum disorders have a different perception of sounds, sights, smell, touch and taste, and this can affect their response to these sensations.

How can the RE teacher help?

- Collaborate closely with parents as they will have many useful strategies.
- Provide visual supports in class: objects, pictures, a symbol timetable, etc.
- Always consider potential sensory issues.
- Give advance warning of any changes to usual routines.

- Provide either an individual desk or the opportunity to work with a buddy.
- Take into account the pupil's individual learning style and preferences.
- Give individual instructions using the pupil's name at the beginning of the request, e.g. 'Paul, bring me your book.'
- Be alert to pupils' levels of anxiety.
- Develop social interactions using a buddy system or Circle of Friends.
- Avoid using metaphor, idiom or sarcasm – say what you mean in simple language.
- Use pupils' special interests as motivations.
- Help pupils to manage potentially difficult situations by rehearsing them beforehand (perhaps with a TA) or through the use of social stories.

Further information

| The National Autistic Society | 020 7833 2299 | www.autism.org.uk |
| Autism Education Trust | 0207 903 3650 | www.autismeducationtrust.org.uk |

Cerebral palsy (CP)

Cerebral palsy is a condition that affects muscle control and movement. It is usually caused by an injury to the brain before, during or after birth. Pupils with cerebral palsy have difficulties in controlling their muscles and movements as they grow and develop. Problems vary from slight clumsiness to more severe lack of control of movements. Pupils with CP may also have learning difficulties. They may use a wheelchair or other mobility aid.

Main characteristics

There are three main forms of cerebral palsy:

- **spastic cerebral palsy** – associated with stiff or tight muscle tone, resulting in a decreased range of movement; this stiffening of muscle tone can be very painful and affect different parts of the body;
- **dyskenetic cerebral palsy** – sustained or intermittent involuntary muscle contractions often affecting the whole body;
- **ataxic cerebral palsy** – an inability to activate the correct pattern of muscles during movement, resulting in an unsteady gait with balance difficulties and poor spatial awareness.

Pupils with CP may also have communication difficulties.

How can the RE teacher help?

- Gather information from parents and therapists involved with the pupil (perhaps via the SENCO until parents' evening provides an opportunity for a face-to-face chat).
- Consider the classroom layout to maximise access.
- Have high academic expectations.
- Use visual supports: objects, pictures, symbols.
- Arrange a work buddy.
- Speak directly to the pupil rather than through a teaching assistant.
- Ensure access to appropriate IT equipment for RE lessons – and check that it is used effectively.

Further information

Scope　　　　0808 800 3333　　　　www.scope.org.uk

Down's syndrome

Down's Syndrome (DS) is the most common identifiable cause of learning disability. This is a genetic condition caused by the presence of an extra chromosome 21. People with DS have varying degrees of learning difficulties ranging from mild to severe. They have a specific learning profile with characteristic strengths and weaknesses. All share certain physical characteristics but will also inherit family traits, in physical features and personality. They may have additional sight, hearing, respiratory and heart problems.

Main characteristics

- delayed motor skills
- taking longer to learn and consolidate new skills
- limited concentration
- difficulties with generalisation, thinking and reasoning
- sequencing difficulties
- stronger visual than aural skills
- better social than academic skills

How can the RE teacher help?

- Ensure that the pupil can see and hear you and other pupils.
- Speak directly to the pupil and reinforce speech with facial expression, pictures and objects.
- Use simple, familiar language in short sentences.
- Check instructions have been understood.
- Give the pupil time to process information and formulate a response.
- Break lessons up into a series of shorter, varied and achievable tasks.
- Accept alternative ways of responding to tasks: drawings, audio or video recordings, symbols, etc.
- Set individual tasks linked to the work of the rest of the class.
- Provide age-appropriate resources and activities.
- Allow the pupil to work with more able peers to give good models of work and behaviour.
- Provide a work buddy.
- Expect pupil to work unsupported for part of every lesson to avoid over-dependence on adult support.

Further information

Down's Syndrome Association   020 8682400   www.downs-syndrome.org.uk

Foetal alcohol syndrome

Foetal alcohol syndrome (FAS) or foetal alcohol spectrum disorders (FASD) are umbrella terms for diagnoses relating to a child's exposure to alcohol before birth. Alcohol can affect the development of all cells and organs, but it is the brain and nervous system that are particularly vulnerable. Each person with FAS/D may face a range of difficulties across a spectrum from mild to severe.

Main characteristics

- visual impairment
- sleep problems
- speech and language delay
- impulsivity and/or hyperactivity
- memory problems
- inappropriate social behaviour

How can the RE teacher help?

- Gather information from parents and other professionals involved with the pupil to find the most effective ways of teaching him/her (perhaps through the SENCO in the first instance).
- Find out the pupil's strengths and use these as starting points for learning.
- Keep instructions simple and offer information in verbal and visual form.
- Ensure class routines are explicit and followed consistently.
- Use concrete and positive language, e.g. 'Walk' rather than 'Don't run'.
- Check the pupil knows and understands any school or class rules.
- Specify clearly what is expected for any task or activity.
- Provide a memory mat or audio recording facilities to support retention of information, e.g. homework tasks, spellings, etc.

Further information

www.drinkaware.co.uk/fas

Learning disability (learning difficulty)

The terms 'learning disability' and 'learning difficulty' are used to describe a wide continuum of difficulties ranging from moderate (MLD) to profound and multiple (PMLD). Pupils with learning disabilities find it harder to understand, learn and remember new things, meaning they may have problems across a range of areas such as communication, being aware of risks or managing everyday tasks.

Moderate learning difficulties (MLD)

The term 'moderate learning difficulties' is used to describe pupils who find it extremely difficult to achieve expected levels of attainment across the curriculum, even with a well-differentiated and flexible approach to teaching. These pupils do not find learning easy and can suffer from low self-esteem and sometimes exhibit unacceptable behaviour as a way of avoiding failure. For all pupils with learning disabilities, the social aspect of school is a crucial element in their development and understanding of the 'culture' of young people, so it is important for them to have friends who don't have learning disabilities as well as those who do. As the SEND Code of Practice says at 6.2 (p. 92): 'Schools must . . . ensure that children and young people with SEN engage in the activities of the school alongside pupils who do not have SEN.'

Main characteristics

- difficulties with reading, writing and comprehension
- problems understanding and retaining mathematical skills and concepts
- immature social and emotional skills
- limited vocabulary and communication skills
- short attention span
- underdeveloped coordination skills
- inability to transfer and apply skills to different situations
- difficulty remembering what has been taught previously
- difficulty with personal organisation such as following a timetable, remembering books and equipment

How can the RE teacher help?

- Find out about the pupil's strengths, interests and areas of weakness.
- Have high expectations.
- Establish a routine within your lessons.
- Keep tasks short and varied.
- Keep listening tasks short or broken up with other activities.
- Provide word lists, writing frames and shortened versions of text to be read.

- Offer alternative methods of recording information, e.g. drawings, charts, labelling, diagrams, use of IT.
- Check previously gained knowledge and build on this (it may be at a very different level from that of other pupils in the class).
- Offer instructions and information in different ways.
- Be explicit about the expected outcome; demonstrate or show examples of completed work.
- Use practical, concrete, visual examples to illustrate explanations.
- Question the pupil to check he has grasped a concept or has understood instructions.
- Make sure the pupil always has something to do.
- Use lots of praise, instant rewards, catch them trying hard.

Severe learning difficulties (SLD)

This term covers a wide and varied group of pupils who have significant intellectual or cognitive impairments. Many have communication difficulties and/ or sensory impairments in addition to more general learning difficulties. Some pupils may also have difficulties in mobility, coordination and perception, and the use of signs and symbols will be helpful to support their communication and understanding. Pupils' academic attainment will also vary, with many able to access a well-differentiated mainstream curriculum and achieve at GCSE level.

How can the RE teacher help?

- Liaise with parents (perhaps through the SENCO in the first instance).
- Arrange a work/subject buddy.
- Use visual supports: objects, pictures, symbols.
- Learn some signs relevant to the teaching of RE.
- Allow time for pupils to process information and formulate responses.
- Set differentiated tasks linked to the work of the rest of the class.
- Set achievable targets for each lesson or module of work.
- Accept different recording methods: drawings, audio or video recordings, photographs, etc.
- Give access to computers where appropriate.
- Plan a series of short, varied activities within each lesson.

Profound and multiple learning difficulties (PMLD)

Pupils with profound and multiple learning difficulties have complex learning needs. In addition to severe learning difficulties, pupils have other significant difficulties, such as physical disabilities, sensory impairments or severe medical conditions. Pupils with PMLD require a high level of adult support, both for their learning needs and for personal care.

Pupils with PMLD are able to access the curriculum largely through sensory experiences. Some pupils communicate by gesture, eye pointing or symbols, others by very simple language. The concept of progress for pupils with PMLD covers more than academic attainment. Indeed, for some pupils who may have associated medical conditions, simply maintaining knowledge and skills will count as good progress.

How can the RE teacher help?

- Work closely with teaching/support assistants working with the pupil.
- Consider the classroom layout so that wheelchairs can move around easily and safely.
- Identify all possible sensory opportunities in your lessons.
- Use additional sensory supports: objects, pictures, fragrances, music, textures, food, etc.
- Use photographs to record the pupil's experiences and responses.
- Set up a work/subject buddy rota for the class.
- Identify opportunities for the pupil to work in groups.

Further information

Mencap	020 7454 0454	www.mencap.org.uk
Foundation for People with Learning Disabilities	020 7803 1100	www.learningdisabilities.org.uk

Physical disability (PD)

There is a wide range of physical disabilities, and pupils with PD span all academic abilities. Some pupils are able to access the curriculum and learn effectively without additional educational provision. They have a disability but do not have a special educational need. For other pupils, the impact of their disability on their education may be significant, and the school will need to make adjustments to enable access to the curriculum.

Some pupils with a physical disability have associated medical conditions that may have an impact on their mobility. These conditions include cerebral palsy, heart disease, spina bifida and muscular dystrophy. They may also have sensory impairments, neurological problems or learning disabilities. They may use a wheelchair and/or additional mobility aids. Some pupils will be mobile but may have significant fine motor difficulties that require support or specialist resources. Others may need augmentative or alternative communication aids.

Pupils with a physical disability may need to miss lessons to attend physiotherapy or medical appointments. They are also likely to become very tired as they expend greater effort to complete everyday tasks. Teachers need to be flexible and sensitive to individual pupil needs.

How can the RE teacher help?

- Get to know the pupil (and parents) so that they will help you make the right adjustments.
- Maintain high expectations.
- Consider the classroom layout.
- Give permission for the pupil to leave lessons a few minutes early to avoid busy corridors and give time to get to next lesson.
- Set homework earlier in the lesson so instructions are not missed.
- Speak directly to pupil rather than through a teaching assistant.
- Let pupils make their own decisions.
- Ensure access to appropriate IT equipment for the lesson – and check that it is used.
- Offer alternative ways of recording work.
- Plan to cover work missed through illness or medical appointments.
- Be sensitive to fatigue, especially towards the end of the school day.

Further information

Scope   0808 800 3333   www.scope.org.uk

Social, emotional and mental health difficulties

This area includes pupils who experience a wide range of difficulties characterised in a number of ways, including becoming withdrawn or exhibiting behavioural difficulties. Behaviours such as these may reflect underlying mental health difficulties including depression, anxiety and eating disorders. These difficulties can be seen across the whole ability range and have a continuum of severity. Attachment disorders and attention deficit disorder will also be part of this continuum. Pupils with special educational needs in this area are those who have persistent difficulties despite the school having in place an effective school behaviour policy and a robust personal and social curriculum.

Main characteristics

- inattentive, poor concentration and lacking interest in school and school work
- easily frustrated and anxious about changes
- difficulty working in groups
- unable to work independently, constantly seeking help or attention
- confrontational: verbally aggressive towards pupils and/or adults
- physically aggressive towards pupils and/or adults
- destroys property: their own and that of others
- appears withdrawn, distressed, unhappy or sulky, and may self-harm
- lacks confidence and self-esteem
- may find it difficult to communicate
- finds it difficult to accept praise

How can the RE teacher help?

- Check the ability level of the pupil and adapt expectations of work accordingly.
- Consider the pupil's strengths and interests and use these as motivators.
- Tell the pupil clearly what you expect in advance, for work and for behaviour.
- Talk to the pupil to find out more about them and how they feel about learning.
- Set a subject target with a reward system.
- Focus your comments on the behaviour not on the pupil ('That was a rude thing to say' rather then 'You are a rude boy').
- Use positive language and gestures and verbal praise whenever possible.
- Tell the pupil what you want them to do: 'I need you to . . .', 'I want you to . . .', rather than asking, 'Will you . . .?'; this avoids confrontation and the possibility that there is room for negotiation.
- Give the pupil a choice between two options.
- Stick to what you say. Be consistent.

- Give the pupil class responsibilities to increase self-esteem and confidence.
- Plan a 'time out' system; ask a colleague for help with this.

Further information

SEBDA   01233 622958   www.sebda.org

Sensory impairments

Hearing impairment (HI)

The term 'hearing impairment' is a generic term used to describe all hearing loss. The main types of loss are monaural, conductive, sensory and mixed loss. The degree of hearing loss is described as mild, moderate, severe or profound.

How can the RE teacher help?

- Find out about the degree of the pupil's hearing loss and the likely implications for your lessons.
- Allocate the most appropriate seating position for the pupil (e g. away from the hum of computers, with the better ear facing towards the speaker).
- Check that the pupil can see your face for facial expressions and lip reading.
- Make sure the light falls on your face and lips. Do not stand with your back to a window.
- Provide a list of vocabulary, context and visual clues, especially for new subjects.
- During class discussion, allow one pupil to speak at a time and indicate where the speaker is.
- Check that any aids are working.
- If you use interactive whiteboards, ensure that the beam does not prevent the pupil from seeing your face.

> **Further information**
>
> | Action on Hearing Loss | 020 7296 8000 | www.actiononhearingloss.org.uk |
> | The National Deaf Children's Society | 020 7490 8656 | www.ndcs.org.uk |

Visual impairment (VI)

Visual impairment refers to a range of difficulties and includes the disabilities of those pupils with monocular vision (vision in one eye), those who are partially sighted and those who are blind. Pupils with visual impairment cover the whole ability range and some pupils may have additional special educational needs.

How can the RE teacher help?

- Check the optimum position for the pupil, e g. for a monocular pupil their good eye should be towards the action.

- Always provide the pupil with his own copy of any texts, with enlarged print where possible.
- Check the accessibility of IT systems (enlarged icons, screen readers, etc.).
- Do not stand with your back to the window as this creates a silhouette and makes it harder for the pupil to see you.
- Draw the pupil's attention to displays – which they may not notice.
- Make sure the floor is kept free of clutter.
- Let the pupil know if there is a change to the layout of a space.
- Ask if there is any specialist equipment that the pupil requires for your subject, such as enlarged print dictionaries or additional lighting.

Further information

Royal National   0303 123 9999   www.rnib.org.uk
Institute for Blind
People RNIB

Multi-sensory impairment (MSI)

Pupils with multi-sensory impairment have a combination of visual and hearing difficulties. They may also have other disabilities that make their situation complex. A pupil with these difficulties is likely to need a high level of individual support.

How can the RE teacher help?

- Liaise with specialist teachers and support staff to ascertain the appropriate provision within your subject.
- Learn how to use alternative means of communication, as appropriate.
- Be prepared to be flexible and to adapt tasks, targets and assessment procedures.

Specific learning difficulties (SpLD)

The term 'specific learning difficulties' includes dyslexia, dyscalculia and dyspraxia.

Dyslexia

The term 'dyslexia' is used to describe difficulties that affect the ability to learn to read, write and/or spell stemming from a difficulty in processing the sounds in words. Although found across a whole range of ability, pupils with dyslexia often have strengths in reasoning and in visual and creative skills, but their particular difficulties can result in underachievement in school. While pupils can learn strategies to manage the effects of dyslexia, it is a life-long condition and its effects may be amplified at times of stress or in unfamiliar situations.

Main characteristics of dyslexia

- The pupil may frequently lose his place while reading, make errors with even high-frequency words and have difficulty reading names, blending sounds and segmenting words. Reading and writing require a great deal of effort and concentration.
- Written work may seem messy, with uneven letters and crossings out. Similarly shaped letters may be confused, such as b/d/p/q, m/w, n/u, and letters in words may be jumbled, such as tired/tried. Spelling difficulties often persist into adult life and these pupils can become reluctant writers.
- Personal organisation can be underdeveloped.

How can the RE teacher help?

- Be aware of the pupil's individual strengths and areas of difficulty – speak to him directly to identify effective support strategies.
- Teach and encourage the use of IT, such as spell-checkers, predictive text, screen readers, etc.
- Provide word lists and photocopies rather than expect the pupil to copy from the board.
- Consider alternatives to lengthy pieces of writing, e.g. pictures, plans, flow charts, mind maps, podcasts, etc.
- Allow extra time for tasks, including assessments and examinations.
- Support the pupil in recording homework to be completed – and time scales.

Further information

www.dyslexiaaction.org.uk

Dyscalculia

The term 'dyscalculia' is used to describe difficulties in processing number concepts and mastering basic numeracy skills. These difficulties might be in marked contrast to the pupil's developmental level and general ability in other areas.

Main characteristics

- The pupil may have difficulty counting by rote, writing or reading numbers, miss out or reverse numbers, have difficulty with mental maths, and be unable to remember concepts, rules and formulae.
- In maths-based concepts, the pupil may have difficulty with money, telling the time, giving/following directions, using right and left and sequencing events. He may also be prone to losing track of turn-taking, e.g. in team games or dance.
- Poor time management and organisation skills.

How can the RE teacher help?

- Provide number/word/rule/formulae lists etc. rather than expect the pupil to copy from the board. (Credit-card holders can be useful for keeping reminders close at hand to aid memory.)
- Make full use of IT to support learning.
- Encourage the use of rough paper for working out.
- Check understanding at regular intervals.
- Offer a framework for setting out work.
- Provide concrete, practical objects that are appropriate for the pupil's age.
- Allow extra time for tasks, including assessments and examinations.

> ### Further information
>
> www.bdadyslexia.org.uk/dyslexic/dyscalculia

Dyspraxia

Dyspraxia is a common developmental disorder that affects fine and gross motor coordination and may also affect speech. The pattern of coordination difficulties will vary from person to person and will affect participation and functioning in everyday life as well as in school.

Main characteristics of dyspraxia

- difficulty in coordinating movements, making pupils appear clumsy
- difficulty with handwriting and drawing, throwing and catching
- confusion between left and right
- difficulty following sequences and multiple instructions
- weak grasp of spatial concepts (in, above, behind, etc.)
- may misinterpret situations, take things literally
- limited social skills, resulting in frustration and irritability
- possible articulation difficulties

How can the RE teacher help?

- Be sensitive to the pupil's limitations in games and practical/outdoor activities and plan tasks to enable success.
- Limit the amount of writing expected.
- Ask the pupil questions to check his understanding of instructions/tasks.
- Check the pupil's seating position to encourage good presentation (both feet resting on the floor, desk at elbow height and ideally with a sloping surface on which to work).

Further information

Dyspraxia Foundation   01462 455 016   www.dyspraxiafoundation.org.uk

Speech, language and communication difficulties (SLCD)

Pupils with speech, language and communication difficulties have problems that affect the full range of communication and the development of skills may be significantly delayed. Such difficulties are very common in young children but most problems are resolved during the primary years. Problems that persist beyond the transfer to secondary school will be more severe and will have a significant effect on self-esteem and personal and social relationships. The development of literacy skills is also likely to be affected. Even where pupils learn to decode, they may not understand what they have read. Sign language and symbols offer pupils an additional method of communication.

Pupils with speech, language and communication difficulties cover the whole range of academic abilities.

Main characteristics

- Speech difficulties: difficulties with expressive language may involve problems in articulation and the production of speech sounds, or in coordinating the muscles that control speech. Pupils may have a stammer or some other form of dysfluency.
- Language/communication difficulties: receptive language impairments lead to difficulty in understanding other people. Pupils may use words incorrectly with inappropriate grammatical patterns, have a reduced vocabulary, or find it hard to recall words and express ideas. Some pupils will also have difficulty using and understanding eye contact, facial expression, gesture and body language.

How can the RE teacher help?

- Gather information about the pupil (perhaps via the SENCO) and talk to the pupil himself about strategies to support him in RE lessons.
- Use visual supports such as objects, pictures, symbols.
- Use the pupil's name when addressing him to alert him to a question or instruction.
- Give one instruction at a time, using short sentences.
- Give pupils time to respond before repeating a question.
- Provide a good model of spoken language and rephrase pupil's response where appropriate: 'I think you are saying that . . .'
- Make sure pupils understand what they have to do before expecting them to start a task.
- Pair with a work buddy.
- Give access to a computer or other IT equipment appropriate to RE lessons.
- Give written homework instructions.

Further information

I CAN	0845 225 4073 or 020 7843 2552	www.ican.org.uk
AFASIC	0300 666 9410 (Helpline)	www.afasic.org.uk

Tourette's syndrome (TS)

Tourette's syndrome is a neurological disorder characterised by 'tics' – involuntary rapid or sudden movements or sounds that are frequently repeated. There is a wide range of severity of the condition, with some people having no need to seek medical help whilst others have a socially disabling condition. The tics can be suppressed for a short time but will be more noticeable when the pupil is anxious or excited.

Main characteristics

- *Physical tics* range from simple blinking or nodding through to more complex movements and conditions such as echopraxia (imitating actions seen) or copropraxia (repeatedly making obscene gestures).
- *Vocal tics* may be as simple as throat clearing or coughing but can progress to be as extreme as echolalia (the repetition of what was last heard) or coprolalia (the repetition of obscene words).

TS itself causes no behavioural or educational problems but pupils may also have other associated disorders such as attention deficit hyperactivity disorder (ADHD) or obsessive compulsive disorder (OCD).

How can the RE teacher help?

- Establish a good rapport with the pupil.
- Talk to the class about TS and establish an understanding and tolerant ethos.
- Agree an 'escape route' signal, should the tics become overwhelming for the pupil or disruptive for the rest of the class.
- Allow pupil to sit at the back of the room to be less obvious.
- Give access to a computer to reduce the need for handwriting.
- Make sure pupil is not teased or bullied.
- Be alert for signs of anxiety or depression.

Further information

Tourettes Action   UK 0300 777 8427   www.tourettes-action.org.uk
                              (Helpdesk)

Appendix 4 P scales

Religious education (DfE 2014)

P1 (i) Pupils encounter activities and experiences

- They may be passive or resistant
- They may show simple reflex responses [for example, startling at sudden noises or movements]
- Any participation is fully prompted.

P1 (ii) Pupils show emerging awareness of activities and experiences

- They may have periods when they appear alert and ready to focus their attention on certain people, events, objects or parts of objects [for example, becoming still in response to silence]
- They may give intermittent reactions [for example, vocalising occasionally during group celebrations and acts of worship].

P2 (i) Pupils begin to respond consistently to familiar people, events and objects

- They react to new activities and experiences [for example, briefly looking around in unfamiliar natural and manmade environments]
- They begin to show interest in people, events and objects [for example, leaning towards the source of a light, sound or scent]
- They accept and engage in coactive exploration [for example, touching a range of religious artefacts and found objects in partnership with a member of staff].

P2 (ii) Pupils begin to be proactive in their interactions

- They communicate consistent preferences and affective responses [for example, showing that they have enjoyed an experience or interaction]

- They recognise familiar people, events and objects [for example, becoming quiet and attentive during a certain piece of music]
- They perform actions, often by trial and improvement, and they remember learned responses over short periods of time [for example, repeating a simple action with an artefact]
- They cooperate with shared exploration and supported participation [for example, performing gestures during ritual exchanges with another person performing gestures].

P3 (i) Pupils begin to communicate intentionally

- They seek attention through eye contact, gesture or action
- They request events or activities [for example, prompting a visitor to prolong an interaction]
- They participate in shared activities with less support. They sustain concentration for short periods
- They explore materials in increasingly complex ways [for example, stroking or shaking artefacts or found objects]
- They observe the results of their own actions with interest [for example, when vocalising in a quiet place]
- They remember learned responses over more extended periods [for example, following a familiar ritual and responding appropriately].

P3 (ii) Pupils use emerging conventional communication

- They greet known people and may initiate interactions and activities [for example, prompting an adult to sing or play a favourite song]
- They can remember learned responses over increasing periods of time and may anticipate known events [for example, celebrating the achievements of their peers in assembly]
- They may respond to options and choices with actions or gestures [for example, choosing to participate in activities]
- They actively explore objects and events for more extended periods [for example, contemplating the flickering of a candle flame]
- They apply potential solutions systematically to problems [for example, passing an artefact to a peer in order to prompt participation in a group activity].

P4 Pupils use single elements of communication [for example, words, gestures, signs or symbols to express their feelings]

- They show they understand 'yes' and 'no'. They begin to respond to the feelings of others [for example, matching their emotions and laugh when another pupil is laughing]

- They join in with activities by initiating ritual actions or sounds. They may demonstrate an appreciation of stillness and quietness.

P5 Pupils respond appropriately to simple questions about familiar religious events or experiences and communicate simple meanings

- They respond to a variety of new religious experiences [for example, involving music, drama, colour, lights, food, or tactile objects]
- They take part in activities involving two or three other learners
- They may also engage in moments of individual reflection.

P6 Pupils express and communicate their feelings in different ways

- They respond to others in group situations and cooperate when working in small groups
- Pupils listen to, and begin to respond to, familiar religious stories, poems and music, and make their own contribution to celebrations and festivals
- They carry out ritualised actions in familiar circumstances
- They show concern and sympathy for others in distress [for example, through gestures, facial expressions or by offering comfort]
- They start to be aware of their own influence on events and other people.

P7 Pupils listen to and follow stories

- They communicate their ideas about religion, life events and experiences in simple phrases
- They evaluate their own work and behaviour in simple ways, beginning to identify some actions as right or wrong on the basis of the consequences
- They find out about aspects of religion through stories, music or drama, answer questions and communicate their responses
- They may communicate their feelings about what is special to them [for example, using role play]
- They begin to understand that other people have needs and to respect these
- They make purposeful relationships with others in group activity.

P8 Pupils listen attentively to religious stories or to people talking about religion

- They begin to understand that religious and other stories carry moral and religious meaning
- They are increasingly able to communicate ideas, feelings or responses to experiences or to retell religious stories
- They communicate simple facts about religion and important people in religions

- They begin to realise the significance of religious artefacts, symbols and places
- They reflect on what makes them happy, sad, excited or lonely
- They demonstrate a basic understanding of what is right and wrong in familiar situations
- They are often sensitive to the needs and feelings of others
- They treat living things and their environment with care and concern.

Appendix 5 Reciprocal discussion

A key aspect of religious education is establishing an environment of mutual respect in the classroom where all pupils feel confident to express their opinions and ask questions.

Arranging seats in a circle can help to create an appropriate atmosphere, and displaying the 'turn-taking rules' helps to remind pupils of your expectations.

The use of 'speech cards' can also be effective. Give out two or three cards to each pupil. They have to 'throw in' a card each time they contribute to the discussion. This can help to discourage individuals from 'wasting' their turn (for example by making disparaging remarks); when their cards have been used, they have used up their 'air-time'. This approach also overcomes the problem of one or two pupils dominating the session. (The 'turn-taking' reminders can also be useful.)

Nominating a member of the group to listen to the discussion and give feedback at the end of the session can also alert pupils to the fact that what they say is being 'recorded'. Ask for a volunteer to do this, or use it as a way of giving responsibility to a particular individual.

Turn-taking

- Listen to the speaker and think about what he is saying.
- Look at the speaker – he may pause and look at you and expect you to speak.
- Wait until the speaker has finished what he is saying before you speak – even if you think you can guess what he is going to say.
- Be fair – everyone should have a chance to speak.
- Keep it short – don't carry on too long – let someone else have a say.

Appendix 6 Spelling

It is important for pupils to build up a working knowledge of key words and technical terms used within each religion, and regular practice of reading and spelling these words will help (little and often). As many different sorts of alphabet are involved, words do not always correspond to our phonetic system and so pupils will need to develop visual memory skills to remember words such as Qur'an, Sikh, Kippah, etc. Displaying words around the room will help to reinforce the spelling of key words, and it may be useful to provide pupils with individual lists to keep in their books/folders. Definition lists can be completed for homework.

As well as the words specific to different faith traditions, there are more generic words which may prove difficult for pupils with special needs to learn, and a little time spent on looking closely at these words, sorting out the 'tricky' bits (the *ie* in 'believe', *h* in 'Christ' and 'Christian', *que* in 'Mosque'); practising the spelling can save time in the long term. The 'look, say, cover, write, check' approach uses all the senses and is especially effective when adopted as a whole-school approach to spelling. Always encourage pupils to 'have a go' at a word they are unsure about – giving them the right number of letters can help; for example, if they ask how to spell 'disciple', the teacher/TA might use a scrap of paper to outline the extent of the word: _ _ _ _ _ _ _ _. Then ask, 'What do you think it begins with?' The pupil usually knows this: d _ _ _ _ _ _ _. Build up the word, using what the pupil knows: d i s _ _ _ l e. Fill in the gaps for him, then encourage the pupil to *look* at the word, *say* it, perhaps trace it in the air, write it – then *cover* it up and try to *write* it from memory. *Check* if it is correct – if not, have another go. This is much more effective than merely telling the pupil how to spell something (which they forget the next time they have need of the word) or making them do spelling corrections by merely copying from a model.

Appendix 7 The writing process

Thinking

- Take some time to think about what to write: what order to do things in (make a plan or mind-map; beginning–middle–end; paragraph headings; subtitles). Make sure you are doing what you have been asked to do.
- Prepare by talking things through (planning on paper if it is complicated).
- Find out what you need to know (make up some questions you need to answer; look in books, in your own notes or on the Internet; ask other people; make observations).

First draft

In jotter or on rough paper.

Revising

Writing often needs redrafting. The changes you make will result in your work becoming clearer, more interesting, more concise or more powerful.

Ask yourself:

- Are things in the right order?
- Do all the sentences mean what I want them to mean?
- Does every word count? Can anything be cut out?
- Are the words well chosen? Can I think of any which are more interesting, more accurate or more unusual?
- Have I repeated the same word, or said the same thing twice, without meaning to?
- Is it legible?
- Is it interesting?
- Is it accurate?
- Have I checked spelling and punctuation?

It is always better to revise your work after a break. Come back to it the next day if possible – you will see it with new eyes and find it easier to make a good assessment. Get someone else to read it and say what they think (if you're brave enough) – or read it aloud to them.

Appendix 8 An RE writing frame

Do Muslims and Christians worship the same God?

A group of Y8 pupils are visiting a local primary school. Your assignment is to to give a short talk to a small group of Y6 pupils at the school on the subject 'Do Muslims and Christians worship the same God?' Use the writing frame below to help you prepare your talk.

> The main beliefs Muslims have about God are that . . .
>
> Muslims also believe that God is . . .
>
> Christians and Muslims have similar views about God, as in both religions they believe . . .
>
> However, Muslims do not believe . . .
>
> Do Muslims and Christians worship the same God? My own view about God is that . . .

Appendix 9 Starter activities

Starter activities should capture the interest of children and get lessons off to a snappy start. They might be used to remind the children about and reinforce the previous lesson or to set up the theme of the forthcoming lesson.

Quiz question

Working in groups of four, each group is asked to come up with five questions and their answers on a particular theme, e.g. five questions about: the fast of Ramadan, how Easter is celebrated, the Jewish Sabbath, the Gurdwara, the story of Rama and Sita, Holy Communion.

What would be missed?

Working in pairs, ask the pupils what would be missed if a particular religious ritual or ceremony was not undertaken. E.g. What would be missed if . . .

- Muslims never went on pilgrimage?
- Buddhists didn't meditate?
- a Christian never prayed?
- the Bible didn't exist?
- Sikhs didn't wear the five Ks?
- Christmas wasn't celebrated?

Who am I?

Ask for a volunteer. Attach a label to the volunteer's head on which is written the name of a person whose life or achievements will be explored in the RE lesson, for example Moses, Desmond Tutu, Muhammad, Mother Teresa, the Buddha, Guru Nanak. The volunteer may ask twenty questions, to which the rest of the class may only answer 'yes' or 'no'. The object of the game is to guess the name on the label before the volunteer runs out of questions.

Snowball

Recall what you can remember learning about in the last RE lesson. Share your ideas with a partner to produce a more accurate account. Now share your ideas in a group of four to produce the most accurate account you can remember. Share your account with the rest of the class.

Appendix 10 A useful model lesson structure

PRESENT the religion being learnt about

If a particular religion features in the lesson, ensure that pupils are clear what religion it is. Make use of a starter which captures the interest of the pupils in the first few minutes of the lesson. Share with the pupils the aims of the lesson. Give children with learning difficulties, or pupils that have a sensory impairment, a copy of any relevant text so that, perhaps with the help of the teaching assistant, they are not slowed down or involved in unproductive copying.

ACTIVE learning strategies

Plan a series of short, varied activities which breaks the lesson up so that the interest of the pupils is retained. Avoid passive activities, like teacher talk or reading. Instead plan more memorable activities which require the pupils to be involved and to do things like act out, speak, report back or move about the classroom. Identify pupils that may not be fully engaged and attempt to involve them so that individuals are not sidelined or feeling left out.

LEARN from religion

Build thinking or reflecting time into most lessons. Identify, or encourage the pupils to identify, what is of value or relevance they can learn from the material being studied. Give pupils an opportunity to consider their own position, or judgement, or perhaps consider what, if anything, they can take away from the lesson which may have application to, or offer insights into, their own life.

DEEPEN and probe

Reinforce and summarise what has been gained from the lesson. Extend and attempt to deepen all of the pupils' thinking and ideas with more probing questions. Encourage pupils to think about their thinking. How well have they presented their ideas, their arguments or reasons? Are there consequences, evidence or scenarios which they have not considered? Is their thinking consistent? Is their reasoning well supported and persuasive? Is there additional evidence to support what they have been saying?

PLENARY and feedback

Allocate plenty of time for the plenary so that it is not rushed at the end. Avoid taking over the plenary and using it as an opportunity for the teacher to tell the children what the teacher believes they have learnt from the lesson. Encourage the pupils to talk about what they learnt or gained from the lesson. Use the plenary as an assessment opportunity to judge how well pupils have understood, what might have to be revisited or better explained, which pupils might need particular support and how best to guide pupils, or structure the scheme of work in the future, in order to maximise learning.

Appendix 11 Guidance for teaching assistants

Golden rules

- Avoid providing answers – allow pupils to think for themselves.
- In RE different views are permitted but disrespectful language is not.
- Avoid too much focus on the who, what and where but instead encourage exploration of the why, the meaning and the significance.
- Avoid giving the impression that world religions are weird, odd or that their primary interest is as an exotic novelty.

Personal information

- In RE you will learn a lot about pupils' beliefs, values, concerns and attitudes.
- Build on and respect personal information and experience.
- RE is very person-centred. Listen to what young people have to say and build a relationship with each child.
- Beware of differences in culture. Use examples which are relevant to the child you are working with. Not all pupils identify with TV soaps, football, pop music and celebrity.

Encourage pupils to participate in class but be aware of individual differences

- Don't just talk; draw, mime, use analogies and examples, and give children quiet thinking time.
- Encourage learning through active strategies such as acting out, demonstrating, reporting back and explaining.
- Try to get each pupil to participate in extended speaking by avoiding questions which require little more than one-word answers. Pose problems which require answers of more length.
- Ensure that the most vocal children do not dominate the lessons. Encourage the quiet or shy (or perhaps the more reflective) pupil to participate and share their views.

- Don't assume that students who are members of a particular religion necessarily always provide the most informed, accurate or wisest insights into that religion.

Appendix 12 Relationships between teachers and TAs

Issues for discussion

- Do all of the RE staff have a clear understanding of the roles and responsibilities of the TA?
- What can they reasonably ask a TA to do?
- Will a TA be expected to work with groups or individuals?
- How are TAs referred to?
- Should they suggest and make additional materials?
- Do you want them to write in pupils' books? If so, should it be in a different colour?
- Are TAs responsible for care needs?
- Will the TA be involved in planning?
- How will the TA feed back information about pupils' progress?
- Does the TA understand the importance of confidentiality?
- Will there be regular meetings between the teacher and TA or HoD and TAs?
- Will TAs be expected to attend staff/departmental meetings?
- Should they provide written notes which could be incorporated into an individual support plan?
- Are TAs responsible for setting up computers and finding other specialist equipment?
- Will opportunities be provided for the TA to source and become familiar with useful hardware and software to meet different teaching needs?
- Will training be available to TAs?
- Will support materials be provided?

Appendix 13 Does prayer work?

<table>
<tr><td>1</td><td>2</td><td>3</td><td>4</td><td>5</td></tr>
</table>

No   Yes

On a scale of 1 to 5 choose the number you most agree with.

Write your number onto a piece of paper (don't sign it).

Put your paper into a box.

Pass the box around and remove one piece of paper.

Place on the floor the numbers 1 to 5.

All those who have a paper with 1 on it stand in line by the number 1 on the floor.

Do the same for the other four numbers until the class has formed a human bar chart of their view about prayer.

Appendix 14 Community of enquiry

Think about the picture quietly.

What question does it raise for you?

My question is . . .

Share your question with a partner and then with two others.

Decide which question you like most.

Our question is . . .

Cut out the question you like most and fix it to the display board.

Appendix 15 The Crucifixion: two views

Look at two different depictions of the Crucifixion, e.g. Matthias Grunewald (dark, sombre, tragic) and Sanzio Raphael (victorious, serene, uplifting).

- Work with a partner. Suggest how artists may have different views about the Crucifixion.
- In a group of four share your ideas.
- As a group of four, agree what the two artists' views might be.
- Which view comes closest to your own opinion? Give your reasons.
- Share your ideas with the rest of the class.

Appendix 16 The Good Samaritan

The Good Samaritan is a famous story Jesus told.

Luke, chapter 10 verses 25–37

What do you think the story tells us?

How might a person be a Good Samaritan today?

I think the story of the Good Samaritan tells us . . .

An example of how a young person could be a Good Samaritan today might be . . .

Appendix 17 What prayer?

1

Dear God
Can you make
us rich? Help
Dad win the lottery.

2

Dear Lord
Please can
I have a new
playstation?

3

Dear God
Make me attractive
like Emma.
Everybody thinks
she is pretty.

4

Dear Lord
Teach us to share
and to help the
hungry and the poor.

5

Dear God
Please guide the
leaders so they can
make the world a
peaceful place.

6

Dear God
Please punish Jake
as he keeps
punching me.

- Cut out the six triangles.
- Arrange the triangles into a pyramid.
- Place the comment you agree with most at the top.
- Place the three you like least at the base of the pyramid.
- Place the two comments which you quite agree with in the middle.
- Give a reason for your answer.

References and useful resources

DfE (2004) 'The Non-statutory National Framework for Religious Education' (NFRE). London: DfE Publications.

DfE (2014) 'Performance – P Scale – Attainment Targets for Pupils with Special Educational Needs', www.gov.uk/government/publications/p-scales-attainment-targets-for-pupils-with-sen

DfE (2015) Special Educational Needs and Disability Code of Practice: 0–25 Years, www.gov.uk/government/publications/send-code-of-practice-0-to-25

Gardner, H. (2011) *Frames of Mind: The Theory of Multiple Intelligences* (3rd edn). London: Basic Books.

Hammond, J., Hay, D., Moxon, J. *et al*. (1990) *New Methods in RE Teaching.* London: Oliver & Boyd.

Ofsted (2013) *Religious Education: Realising the Potential,* www.secularism.org.uk/uploads/religious-education-realising-the-potential.pdf

QCA (2000) 'Religious Education: Non-statutory Guidance on RE', QCA/00/576, www.re-handbook.org.uk/media/display/religious_education_non-statuory_guidance.pdf

Religious Education Council (REC) (2013) 'A Review of Religious Education in England', www.areiac.org.uk/public/downloads/NCFRE.pdf

Useful resources

Association for Religious Education Inspectors, Advisers and Consultants (AREIAC). Publishes guidance on inspections and syllabuses etc.

www.areiac.org.uk

National Association of Teachers of Religious Education. UK subject teacher association for RE professionals in primary and secondary schools and higher education; includes news, resources, magazine articles.

www.natre.org.uk

NASACRE works to support, strengthen and promote the work done by local SACREs and represents the interests of members at a national level.

www.nasacre.org.uk

The Religious Education Council of England and Wales provides a multi-faith forum to support and promote religious education in schools and colleges.

www.religiouseducationcouncil.org.uk

The RE site provides links to places of worship, resources and information.

www.theresite.org.uk

Online resources also at:

www.reonline.org.uk
www.hindukids.org

Index